T0243445

THE
COMFORT FOOD
COOKBOOK

THE COMFORT FOOD COOKBOOK

13-Digit ISBN: 978-1-64643-276-9
10-Digit ISBN: 1-64643-276-2

This book may be ordered by mail from the publisher. Please include $5.99 for postage and handling. Please support your local bookseller first!

Books published by Cider Mill Press Book Publishers are available at special discounts for bulk purchases in the United States by corporations, institutions, and other organizations. For more information, please contact the publisher.

Cider Mill Press Book Publishers
"Where good books are ready for press"
501 Nelson Place
Nashville, Tennessee 37214

cidermillpress.com

Typography: Area Normal, Farmhand

Image Credits: Pages 19, 23, 24, 31, 35, 78–79, 82, 91, 92, 95, 96, 99, 107, 111, 115, 119, 121, 159, 160, 164, 167, 175, 176, 179, 180, 184, 191, 196, 215, and 216 courtesy of Cider Mill Press. Page 132 courtesy of Stockfood. All other photos used under official license from Shutterstock.com.

Front cover image: Roasted Chicken, see page 133.

Printed in Malaysia

23 24 25 26 27 OFF 5 4 3 2 1
First Edition

THE
COMFORT FOOD
COOKBOOK

OVER 100 DELICIOUS RECIPES
THAT TASTE LIKE HOME

CIDER MILL
PRESS

BOOK
PUBLISHERS

CONTENTS

INTRODUCTION

In the course of a year, there will invariably be a few moments where you or a loved one will need a little pick-me-up, occasions when the chaos of the world grinds us down, when every single thing we need or want feels out of reach.

At these times, something that can ground, calm, and nourish is required. And while the power of a hug and a few words of encouragement should never be overlooked, there is truly nothing that can remove the clouds from our eyes and remind us of all the good the world and our lives contain like a plate or bowl of some warm and lovingly prepared food.

Comfort foods, as these balms have come to be known, can take on a number of forms. Sometimes they will remind us of simpler times, as a grilled cheese or a slice of pizza does, evoking fond memories of childhood. At others, a warm bowl of soup or a luscious confection is required to ease our burden.

Whatever form they end up taking, comfort foods do share a few characteristics—they are rich to the point of seeming decadent and easy to prepare. Once these requirements are met, there are no real restrictions on what can serve as a comfort food. They are found in each and every cuisine across the globe, present in every approach to eating, whether gluten-free, vegan, vegetarian, or keto.

Though they are almost always humble and accessible, comfort foods are, in the end, invaluable. To recognize this reality, we've collected some of the very best dishes in one place so that, in those moments where your brain feels ready to break, you don't even have to think about where to turn—you can just blindly reach to the shelf where you keep this book and instantaneously feel the relief that attends the recognition that this too will pass—and soon.

BREAKFAST & BREADS

There's never a convenient time to be in need of comfort. But it's an especially unwelcome feeling in the morning, as it threatens to throw the entire day out of whack. These breakfast dishes ensure that you can navigate these turbulent times easily and set your house in order.

And, if you're one of those people who craves something carb-laden when the chips are down, a handful of delicious bread recipes are here to help.

CHEESY HASH BROWNS

INGREDIENTS

4 large russet potatoes, peeled and shredded

4 tablespoons unsalted butter

1 teaspoon kosher salt

Black pepper, to taste

6 eggs

½ cup milk

1 cup shredded cheddar cheese

1   Preheat the oven to 375°F. Place the potatoes in a linen towel and wring the towel to remove as much moisture from the potatoes as possible. Place the potatoes in a bowl.

2   Place the butter in a large cast-iron skillet and melt it over medium-high heat. Add the potatoes and salt and season with pepper. Press down on the potatoes to ensure they are in an even layer. Cook the potatoes, without stirring, for 5 minutes.

3   In a mixing bowl, whisk the eggs and milk until combined. Pour the mixture over the potatoes and shake the pan to help the egg mixture penetrate to the bottom. Sprinkle the cheese on top and then transfer the skillet to the oven.

4   Bake until the cheese is melted and golden brown, about 10 minutes. Remove the skillet from the oven and enjoy.

SPANISH TORTILLA

INGREDIENTS

5 large russet potatoes, peeled and sliced thin

1 Spanish onion, sliced

½ cup canola oil, plus more as needed

½ cup extra-virgin olive oil

10 eggs, at room temperature

Large pinch of kosher salt

1   Place the potatoes, onion, canola oil, and olive oil in a large cast-iron skillet. The potatoes should be submerged. If not, add more canola oil as needed. Bring to a gentle simmer over low heat and cook until the potatoes are tender, about 30 minutes. Remove the pan from heat and let cool slightly.

2   Use a slotted spoon to remove the potatoes and onion from the oil. Pour the oil into a measuring cup and reserve it.

3   Place the eggs and salt in a large bowl and whisk until scrambled. Stir the potatoes and onion into the eggs.

4   Warm the skillet over high heat. Add ¼ cup of the reserved oil and swirl to coat the bottom and sides of the pan. Pour the egg-and-potato mixture into the pan and stir vigorously to ensure that the mixture does not stick to the side. Cook for 1 minute and remove the pan from heat. Place the pan over low heat, cover it, and cook for 3 minutes.

5   Carefully invert the tortilla onto a large plate. Return the tortilla to the skillet, cook for 3 minutes, and then invert it onto the plate. Return it to the skillet and cook for another 3 minutes. Remove the tortilla from the pan and let it rest at room temperature for 1 hour before serving.

HUEVOS RANCHEROS

INGREDIENTS

¾ cup extra-virgin olive oil

4 corn tortillas

3 large tomatoes, cut into several big pieces

¼ onion, peeled

2 serrano chile peppers, stems and seeds removed, sliced

Salt, to taste

4 eggs

½ lb. queso fresco, shredded, for garnish

½ cup chopped fresh cilantro, for garnish

Black beans, for serving

1 Place half of the olive oil in a large skillet and warm it over medium-high heat. Add the tortillas one at a time and fry for about 1 minute on each side. Transfer the tortillas to a paper towel-lined plate and let them drain.

2 Place the tomatoes, onion, and chiles in a blender and puree until smooth.

3 Place 2 tablespoons of the remaining olive oil in a small skillet and warm it over medium heat. Carefully add the puree, reduce the heat to low, and cook for 5 minutes. Season the salsa with salt and then set it aside.

4 Place the remaining oil in a skillet, add the eggs, season the yolks generously with salt, and fry them to the desired level of doneness.

5 To assemble, place an egg on top of a fried tortilla, spoon the salsa on top, and garnish with the cheese and cilantro. Serve with black beans and enjoy.

BUTTERMILK WAFFLES

INGREDIENTS

2 cups all-purpose flour

2 tablespoons sugar

2 teaspoons baking powder

½ teaspoon kosher salt

2 cups buttermilk

½ cup unsalted butter, melted

2 eggs

1   Preheat a waffle iron and preheat the oven to 160°F. Place the flour, sugar, baking powder, and salt in a large bowl and whisk to combine.

2   Place the remaining ingredients in a separate mixing bowl, whisk to combine, and add the wet mixture to the dry mixture. Whisk until the mixture comes together as a smooth batter.

3   Working in batches, pour the batter into the waffle iron, close it, and cook until the waffle is browned and crispy. Place the cooked waffles on a platter and keep them warm in the oven until all of the batter has been used.

BUTTERMILK WAFFLES, SEE PAGE 15

PEANUT BUTTER & BACON OATS

INGREDIENTS

6 slices of thick-cut bacon

6 eggs

2 cups steel-cut oats

6 cups water

1 tablespoon kosher salt

¼ cup crunchy peanut butter

1 Place the bacon in a large cast-iron skillet and cook over medium heat until it is crispy, about 8 minutes. Transfer the bacon to a paper towel–lined plate, add the eggs to the skillet, and fry them in the bacon fat. Transfer the eggs to a plate and cover it loosely with aluminum foil to keep the eggs warm.

2 Wipe out the skillet, add the oats, water, and salt and cook over medium heat until the oats are tender, 10 to 15 minutes.

3 While the oats are cooking, chop the bacon. Add the bacon and peanut butter to the oats and stir to incorporate. Ladle the oatmeal into warmed bowls, top each portion with a fried egg, and enjoy.

BLUEBERRY MUFFINS

INGREDIENTS

20 oz. all-purpose flour

1 tablespoon baking powder

1½ teaspoons kosher salt

½ lb. unsalted butter, softened

10 oz. sugar

6 eggs

½ cup sour cream

11 oz. milk

2 cups fresh blueberries

1 Preheat the oven to 375°F and line a 12-well muffin pan with paper liners.

2 Place the flour, baking powder, and salt in a mixing bowl and whisk to combine. Set the mixture aside.

3 In the work bowl of a stand mixer fitted with the paddle attachment, cream the butter and sugar on medium until the mixture is light and fluffy, about 5 minutes. Add the eggs and beat until incorporated. Add the dry mixture, reduce the speed to low, and beat until the mixture comes together as a smooth batter. Add the sour cream and beat until incorporated. Gradually add the milk and beat to incorporate. Add the blueberries, reduce the speed to low, and beat until evenly distributed.

4 Pour ½ cup of muffin batter into each liner. Place the pan in the oven and bake the muffins until a knife inserted into the center of each one comes out clean, 20 to 25 minutes.

5 Remove the muffins from the oven, place the pan on a wire rack, and let the muffins cool completely before enjoying.

BANANA & CHOCOLATE CHIP MUFFINS

INGREDIENTS

2 cups all-purpose flour

1 teaspoon baking soda

¼ teaspoon cinnamon

¼ teaspoon freshly grated nutmeg

½ teaspoon kosher salt

3 ripe bananas, peeled

4 oz. light brown sugar

6 oz. sugar

2 oz. unsalted butter, softened

½ cup extra-virgin olive oil

2 eggs

1½ teaspoons pure vanilla extract

2 tablespoons sour cream

1 cup semisweet chocolate chips

1   Preheat the oven to 350°F and line a 12-well muffin pan with paper liners.

2   Place the flour, baking soda, cinnamon, nutmeg, and salt in a mixing bowl and whisk to combine. Set the mixture aside.

3   In the work bowl of a stand mixer fitted with the paddle attachment, beat the bananas, brown sugar, sugar, and butter on medium for 5 minutes. Add the olive oil, eggs, and vanilla and beat until incorporated. Add the dry mixture, reduce the speed to low, and beat until the mixture comes together as a smooth batter. Add the sour cream and chocolate chips and beat until incorporated.

4   Pour ½ cup of muffin batter into each liner, place the pan in the oven, and bake the muffins until a knife inserted into the center of each one comes out clean, 20 to 22 minutes.

5   Remove the muffins from the oven, place the pan on a wire rack, and let the muffins cool completely before enjoying.

HAM & CHEESE CROISSANTS

INGREDIENTS

1 sheet of frozen puff pastry, thawed

⅔ cup Dijon mustard

16 slices of smoked ham

16 slices of Swiss cheese

1 egg, beaten

1   Preheat the oven to 400°F and line two baking sheets with parchment paper. Roll out the sheet of puff pastry until it is very thin. Using a pizza cutter or a chef's knife, cut the puff pastry into 8 rectangles and then cut each rectangle diagonally, yielding 16 triangles. Gently roll out each triangle until it is 8 inches long.

2   Spread 2 teaspoons of the mustard toward the wide side of each triangle. Lay a slice of ham over the mustard and top it with a slice of cheese, making sure to leave 1 inch of dough uncovered at the tip.

3   Roll the croissants up tight, moving from the wide sides of the triangles to the tips. Tuck the tips under the croissants. Place 8 croissants on each of the baking sheets.

4   Place the croissants in the oven and bake until they are golden brown, 20 to 22 minutes. Remove the croissants from the oven and place them on wire racks. Let the croissants cool slightly before enjoying.

CHICKEN CONGEE

INGREDIENTS

4 chicken legs, skin removed

4 cups Chicken Stock
(see page 237)

1 teaspoon turmeric

2 tablespoons extra-virgin olive
oil

1 garlic clove, minced

1½ cups long-grain rice

Salt and pepper, to taste

Fresh cilantro, chopped, for
garnish

1   Place the chicken, stock, and turmeric in a Dutch oven and bring to a simmer over medium heat. Simmer until the chicken is cooked through, about 15 minutes.

2   Using a slotted spoon, remove the chicken, set it aside, and allow the stock to continue simmering. When the chicken is cool enough to handle, remove the meat from the bones, shred it into bite-sized pieces, and discard the bones.

3   Place the olive oil in a large skillet and warm it over medium heat. Add the garlic and cook until it is fragrant and golden brown. Add the rice, stir to coat, and cook until the rice is golden brown, about 4 minutes.

4   Add the rice and garlic to the stock and season it with salt and pepper. Cook, stirring occasionally, until the rice is creamy and tender, about 20 minutes.

5   Stir the shredded chicken into the pot and cook until it is warmed through.

6   Ladle the congee into warmed bowls, garnish with cilantro, and enjoy.

EVERYTHING BAGELS

INGREDIENTS

For the Dough

6 oz. water

¼ cup honey

1 egg white

1 tablespoon canola oil

2 teaspoons active dry yeast

1½ oz. sugar

19 oz. bread flour, plus more as needed

1½ teaspoons kosher salt

1 egg, beaten

For the Bath

½ cup honey

For the Everything Seasoning

2 tablespoons poppy seeds

1 tablespoon fennel seeds

1 tablespoon onion flakes

1 tablespoon garlic flakes

2 tablespoons sesame seeds

1 To begin preparations for the dough, place the water, honey, egg white, and canola oil in the work bowl of a stand mixer fitted with the dough hook and whisk to combine. Add the yeast, sugar, flour, and salt and work the mixture for 1 minute on low. Raise the speed to medium and knead the mixture until it comes together as a smooth dough and pulls away from the side of the work bowl, about 10 minutes.

2 Place the dough on a flour-dusted work surface and shape it into a ball. Return the dough to the work bowl, cover it with plastic wrap, and let the dough rise at room temperature until it has doubled in size.

3 Divide the dough into six 5-oz. pieces and form each one into a ball.

4 Coat an 18 x 13-inch baking sheet with nonstick cooking spray. Place the pieces of dough on the pan, cover them with plastic wrap, and let them rise until they have doubled in size.

5 Using your fingers, make a small hole in the centers of the balls of dough. Place both of your index fingers in the holes and, working in a rotating motion, slowly stretch the pieces of dough into 4-inch-wide bagels. Place the bagels on the baking sheet, cover them with plastic wrap, and let them sit for 30 minutes.

6 Preheat the oven to 350°F. To prepare the bath, combine 12 cups of water with the honey in a wide saucepan and bring to a boil.

7 Gently place the bagels in the boiling water and poach them on each side for 30 seconds. Remove the bagels from the water and place them back on the baking sheet.

8 To prepare the everything seasoning, place all of the ingredients in a mixing bowl and stir to combine. Brush the bagels with the egg and sprinkle the seasoning over them.

9 Place the bagels in the oven and bake until they are a deep golden brown, 20 to 25 minutes.

10 Remove the pan from the oven, place the bagels on a wire rack, and let them cool before enjoying.

EVERYTHING BAGELS, SEE PAGE 27

RUM & CARAMELIZED BANANA BREAD

INGREDIENTS

2 cups all-purpose flour

1 teaspoon baking soda

¼ teaspoon cinnamon

¼ teaspoon allspice

½ teaspoon kosher salt

4 tablespoons unsalted butter, softened

3½ ripe bananas, peeled and sliced

4 oz. light brown sugar

2 tablespoons spiced rum

6 oz. sugar

½ cup extra-virgin olive oil

2 eggs

1½ teaspoons pure vanilla extract

2 tablespoons crème fraîche

1 Preheat the oven to 350°F. Coat an 8 x 4-inch loaf pan with nonstick cooking spray.

2 Place the flour, baking soda, cinnamon, allspice, and salt in a mixing bowl and whisk to combine. Set the mixture aside.

3 Place the butter in a large skillet and melt it over medium heat. Add the bananas and brown sugar and cook, stirring occasionally, until the bananas start to brown, about 3 minutes. Remove the pan from heat, stir in the rum, and let the mixture steep for 30 minutes.

4 In the work bowl of a stand mixer fitted with the paddle attachment, cream the caramelized banana mixture, sugar, olive oil, eggs, and vanilla on medium for 5 minutes. Add the dry mixture, reduce the speed to low, and beat until the mixture comes together as a smooth batter. Add the crème fraîche and beat to incorporate.

5 Pour the batter into the loaf pan, place it in the oven, and bake until a cake tester inserted into the center of the loaf comes out clean, 60 to 70 minutes.

6 Remove the pan from the oven, place it on a wire rack, and let the banana bread cool completely before enjoying.

FOCACCIA

INGREDIENTS

For the Poolish

3¼ cups water

2 tablespoons active dry yeast

½ cup sugar

½ cup plus 2 tablespoons extra-virgin olive oil

For the Dough

28 oz. bread flour

20 oz. all-purpose flour

2 tablespoons finely chopped fresh rosemary

1 tablespoon finely chopped fresh thyme

2 tablespoons finely chopped fresh basil

3 tablespoons kosher salt

1½ teaspoons black pepper

1½ cups extra-virgin olive oil, plus more as needed

1 cup freshly shaved Parmesan cheese

1 To prepare the poolish, place all the ingredients in a mixing bowl and whisk to combine. Cover the bowl with a linen towel and let it sit at room temperature for 30 minutes.

2 To begin preparations for the dough, place the poolish in the work bowl of a stand mixer fitted with the dough hook. Add all the remaining ingredients, except for the olive oil and Parmesan, and work the mixture on low for 1 minute. Raise the speed to medium and knead the mixture until it comes together as a smooth dough, about 5 minutes. Cover the bowl with a linen towel and let the dough rise until it has doubled in size.

3 Preheat the oven to 350°F.

4 Coat an 18 x 13-inch baking sheet with olive oil and place the dough on the pan. Use your fingers to gradually stretch the dough until it fills the entire pan and is as even as possible. If the dough is difficult to stretch, let it rest for 10 minutes before resuming.

5 Cover the dough with plastic wrap and let it rise at room temperature until it has doubled in size.

6 Use your fingertips to gently press down on the dough and make dimples all over it. The dimples should go about halfway down. Drizzle about 1 cup of olive oil over the focaccia and sprinkle the Parmesan on top.

7 Place the focaccia in the oven and bake until it is a light golden brown, 20 to 30 minutes.

8 Remove the focaccia from the oven and brush it generously with the remaining olive oil. Let it cool slightly before slicing and serving.

PIDES

1 To begin preparations for the dough, place all of the ingredients in the work bowl of a stand mixer fitted with the dough hook and work the mixture until it comes together as a smooth dough.

2 Coat a bowl with olive oil. Place the dough on a flour-dusted work surface and knead it for 2 minutes. Form the dough into a ball and place it, seam side down, in the bowl. Cover with a linen towel and let the dough rise in a warm spot until it has doubled in size, about 1 hour.

3 To begin preparations for the filling, place 2 tablespoons of the olive oil in a large saucepan and warm it over medium heat. Add the eggplant and cook, stirring occasionally, until it has browned and is soft, about 5 minutes. Remove the pan from heat and set the eggplant aside.

4 Place 1 tablespoon of the olive oil in a clean large saucepan and warm it over medium heat. Add the onion and bell pepper and cook, stirring occasionally, until softened, about 5 minutes. Add the garlic, red pepper flakes, and paprika and cook, stirring continually, for 1 minute.

5 Add the tomatoes and bring to a boil. Reduce the heat and simmer until the tomatoes start to collapse, about 10 minutes, mashing them with a wooden spoon as they cook.

6 Stir in the eggplant and cook until warmed through. Season the mixture with salt and pepper, remove the pan from heat, and let the mixture cool.

7 Preheat the oven to 450°F. Line two baking sheets with parchment paper. Cut four 12 x 4-inch strips of parchment. Divide the dough into four pieces and place each one on a piece of parchment. Roll out the dough until each extends ½ inch over the parchment on all sides.

8 Spread the eggplant mixture over the pieces of dough, leaving a 1-inch border on the sides. Sprinkle the feta over the eggplant and brush the border with some of the remaining olive oil.

9 Fold each side toward the center, leaving about 1 inch of the filling exposed. Pinch the bottoms of the pides to secure them, brush the dough with some of the remaining olive oil, and sprinkle the Maldon sea salt over the top.

10 Place the pides in the oven and bake until the edges are crispy and golden brown, about 12 minutes. Remove the pides from the oven and let them cool slightly before garnishing with mint and serving.

INGREDIENTS

For the Dough

2 cups plus 2 tablespoons bread flour, plus more as needed

1 teaspoon sugar

¼ teaspoon instant yeast

⅔ cup plus 2 tablespoons warm water (105°F)

1 teaspoon fine sea salt

2 teaspoons extra-virgin olive oil, plus more as needed

For the Filling

¼ cup extra-virgin olive oil

4 cups diced eggplant (¼-inch cubes)

2 tablespoons white wine

1 onion, chopped

½ red bell pepper, diced

2 garlic cloves, minced

⅛ teaspoon red pepper flakes

½ teaspoon paprika

1 (28 oz.) can of whole peeled San Marzano tomatoes, drained

Salt and pepper, to taste

1 cup crumbled feta cheese

1 teaspoon Maldon sea salt

Fresh mint, chopped, for garnish

HONEY CORNBREAD

INGREDIENTS

½ cup honey

¾ lb. unsalted butter, softened

1 lb. all-purpose flour

½ lb. cornmeal

1 tablespoon plus 1 teaspoon baking powder

1 tablespoon kosher salt

7 oz. sugar

4 eggs

2 cups milk

1 Preheat the oven to 350°F. Coat a 13 x 9-inch baking pan with nonstick cooking spray.

2 Place the honey and 4 oz. of the butter in a small saucepan and warm over medium heat until the butter has melted. Whisk to combine and set the mixture aside.

3 Place the flour, cornmeal, baking powder, and salt in a mixing bowl and whisk to combine. Set the mixture aside.

4 In the work bowl of a stand mixer fitted with the paddle attachment, cream the remaining butter and the sugar on medium until light and fluffy, about 5 minutes. Add the eggs and beat until incorporated. Add the dry mixture, reduce the speed to low, and beat until the mixture comes together as a smooth batter. Gradually add the milk and beat until incorporated.

5 Pour the batter into the pan, place the pan in the oven, and bake until a cake tester inserted into the center of the cornbread comes out clean, 25 to 30 minutes.

6 Remove from the oven and place the pan on a wire rack. Brush the cornbread with the honey butter and enjoy it warm.

APPETIZERS & SNACKS

When the pressure is bearing down, something fast, comforting, and classic is required. This chapter has you covered in these seemingly desperate moments, collecting delicious, easy-to-prepare recipes that will quickly soothe any anxieties with their decadent and accessible tastes.

SOFT PRETZELS

INGREDIENTS

½ cup warm water (105°F)

2 tablespoons brown sugar

¼ teaspoon instant yeast

6 tablespoons unsalted butter, melted

2½ teaspoons fine sea salt

4½ cups all-purpose flour

⅓ cup baking soda

1 egg

1 tablespoon water, at room temperature

Coarse sea salt, to taste

1 In the work bowl of a stand mixer fitted with the dough hook, combine the warm water, brown sugar, yeast, and melted butter and mix on low for 5 minutes.

2 Add the fine sea salt and flour, raise the speed to medium, and knead for 4 minutes. Coat a large mixing bowl with nonstick cooking spray, transfer the dough to the bowl, and cover it with plastic wrap. Let the dough rest at room temperature until it has doubled in size, about 1 hour.

3 Cut the dough into ½-inch-thick ropes. Cut the ropes into bite-sized pieces or twist them into traditional pretzel shapes.

4 Preheat the oven to 425°F. Line two baking sheets with parchment paper and coat with nonstick cooking spray. Bring water to a boil in a medium saucepan. Gradually add the baking soda and gently stir to combine.

5 Place the pretzels in the water and poach them briefly—30 seconds for bites, 1 minute for traditional pretzels. Carefully remove the pretzels with a slotted spoon and transfer them to the baking sheets.

6 Place the egg and room-temperature water in a small bowl, beat to combine, and brush the egg wash over the pretzels. Sprinkle coarse sea salt over the pretzels and bake them in the oven until golden brown, about 15 minutes.

7 Remove the pretzels from the oven and briefly let them cool before serving.

STUFFED MUSHROOMS

INGREDIENTS

10 oz. button mushrooms, stemmed

¼ cup extra-virgin olive oil, plus more as needed

3 tablespoons balsamic vinegar

Salt and pepper, to taste

½ lb. ground Italian sausage

2 yellow onions, grated

5 garlic cloves, grated

½ lb. cream cheese, softened

1 cup shredded Asiago cheese

Bread crumbs, for topping

Fresh parsley, chopped, for topping

1 Place the mushrooms, olive oil, and balsamic vinegar in a mixing bowl and toss to coat. Season the mixture with salt and pepper and then place it on a baking sheet. Place in the oven and bake until the mushrooms are just starting to brown, about 25 minutes. Remove from the oven and set them aside.

2 Coat the bottom of a large skillet with olive oil and warm it over medium heat. When the oil starts to shimmer, add the sausage and cook, breaking it up with a fork as it browns, until cooked through, about 8 minutes. Remove the sausage from the pan and place it in a mixing bowl.

3 Preheat the oven to 375°F. Place the onions in the skillet, reduce the heat to medium-low, and cook until dark brown, about 15 minutes. Stir in the garlic, sauté for 1 minute, and then add the mixture to the bowl containing the sausage. Add the cheeses and stir to combine.

4 Arrange the mushrooms on the baking sheet so that their cavities are facing up. Fill the cavities with the sausage mixture, top it with bread crumbs and parsley, the mushrooms in the oven, and bake until the cheese has melted and is golden brown, about 25 minutes. Remove from the oven and let cool slightly before serving.

YIELD: 6 SERVINGS • ACTIVE TIME: 20 MINUTES • TOTAL TIME: 35 MINUTES

SOUTHWESTERN SLIDERS

INGREDIENTS

1 large egg

2 chipotle chile peppers in adobo

2 tablespoons whole milk

½ cup bread crumbs

½ cup grated jalapeño jack cheese

3 tablespoons finely chopped fresh cilantro

3 tablespoons canned diced green chilies, drained

4 garlic cloves, minced

1 tablespoon dried oregano

1 tablespoon smoked paprika

2 teaspoons cumin

1¼ lbs. ground beef

Salt and pepper, to taste

Slider rolls, for serving

1 Preheat a gas or charcoal grill to medium-high heat (about 450°F). Place the egg, chipotles, milk, and bread crumbs in a food processor and puree until smooth. Place the mixture in a mixing bowl, add the cheese, cilantro, green chilies, garlic, oregano, paprika, and cumin and stir until thoroughly combined.

2 Stir in the beef and season the mixture with salt and pepper. Working with wet hands, form the mixture into 3-inch patties. Place the sliders on the grill and cook until they are cooked through, about 10 minutes, flipping them over once. Remove the sliders from the grill, transfer them to a platter, and tent them loosely with aluminum foil.

3 Let the sliders rest for 10 minutes before serving with the slider rolls and your favorite burger fixings.

POUTINE

INGREDIENTS

Canola oil, as needed

2 russet potatoes, cut into long, thin fries

Salt and pepper, to taste

4 tablespoons unsalted butter

¼ cup all-purpose flour

1 garlic clove, minced

4 cups Beef Stock (see page 239)

2 tablespoons ketchup

1 tablespoon apple cider vinegar

1½ teaspoons Worcestershire sauce

2 cups cheese curds

1 Add canola oil to a Dutch oven until it is about 2 inches deep and warm it to 275°F. Gently slip the potatoes into the hot oil and fry for 5 minutes, stirring occasionally. Use a slotted spoon to remove the potatoes, transfer them to a paper towel-lined plate, and let them cool completely.

2 Warm the canola oil to 350°F. Return the cooled, once-fried potatoes to the hot oil and fry until they are crispy and golden brown, about 5 minutes, stirring occasionally. Transfer the French fries to a paper towel-lined plate and season them with salt. Once the fries have drained, place them in a serving dish.

3 Place the butter in a medium saucepan and melt it over medium-high heat. Add the flour and cook, stirring continually, until the mixture is smooth, about 2 minutes.

4 Add the garlic and cook until it has softened, about 2 minutes. Stir in the stock, ketchup, vinegar, and Worcestershire sauce, season the mixture with salt and pepper, and bring to a boil. Cook, stirring frequently, until the gravy has thickened, about 6 minutes.

5 Remove the pan from heat and pour the gravy over the fries. Top with the cheese curds and enjoy immediately.

BUFFALO WINGS WITH BLUE CHEESE DRESSING

INGREDIENTS

4 tablespoons unsalted butter

1 tablespoon white vinegar

¾ cup hot sauce

1 teaspoon cayenne pepper

Canola oil, as needed

2 lbs. chicken wings

1 cup cornstarch

Salt, to taste

¼ cup sour cream

¼ cup mayonnaise

¼ cup buttermilk

1 tablespoon fresh lemon juice

Pinch of black pepper

1 cup crumbled blue cheese

Celery sticks, for serving

1 Place the butter in a large saucepan and melt it over medium heat. When it has melted, whisk in the vinegar, hot sauce, and cayenne, making sure not to breathe in the spicy steam. Remove the pan from heat and cover the sauce to keep it warm.

2 Add canola oil to a large Dutch oven until it is about 2 inches deep and gradually warm it to 375°F over medium heat.

3 Pat the chicken wings dry and dredge them in the cornstarch until completely coated. Working in batches to avoid crowding the pot, gently slip the chicken wings into the hot oil and fry until they are golden brown and crispy, about 10 minutes. Transfer the fried chicken wings to a wire rack and season them with salt.

4 Add the fried chicken wings to the spicy sauce in the saucepan and toss until they are coated. Remove them with a slotted spoon and arrange them on a platter.

5 Place the sour cream, mayonnaise, buttermilk, lemon juice, and black pepper in a bowl and whisk to combine. Add the blue cheese, stir to incorporate, and serve the blue cheese dressing and celery alongside the chicken wings.

YIELD: 4 SERVINGS • ACTIVE TIME: 10 MINUTES • TOTAL TIME: 30 MINUTES

PROSCIUTTO-WRAPPED FIGS

INGREDIENTS

12 thin slices of prosciutto

6 ripe figs, halved lengthwise

Aged balsamic vinegar, to taste

1 Preheat a gas or charcoal grill to high heat (500°F). Wrap a slice of the prosciutto tightly around each fig half and place them on the grill, cut side down. Cook the figs until they are browned and crispy all over, 2 to 3 minutes per side.

2 Transfer the figs to a platter, drizzle balsamic vinegar over the top, and serve.

FRIED SQUASH BLOSSOMS

INGREDIENTS

10 squash blossoms, stamens removed

1 bunch of fresh spearmint

2 cups shredded queso fresco

Zest and juice of 1 lemon

Salt, to taste

1 cup all-purpose flour

1 teaspoon baking powder

2 egg yolks

1 cup seltzer water

2 cups canola oil

1   Place the squash blossoms on a paper towel–lined baking sheet.

2   Finely chop the spearmint and combine it with the queso fresco. Add the lemon zest and juice, season the mixture with salt, and stir to combine.

3   Stuff the squash blossoms with the mixture, taking care not to tear the flowers.

4   In a small bowl, combine the flour, baking powder, egg yolks, and seltzer water and work the mixture with a whisk until it is a smooth batter. Let the batter rest for 20 minutes.

5   Place the canola oil in a deep skillet and warm it to 350°F.

6   Fold the tips of the squash blossoms closed and dip them into the batter until evenly coated. Working in batches to avoid crowding the pan, gently slip them into the hot oil and fry until crispy and golden brown all over, about 2 minutes, making sure you only turn the squash blossoms once.

7   Drain the fried squash blossoms on the baking sheet. Season them lightly with salt and enjoy.

FRIED SQUASH BLOSSOMS, SEE PAGE 51

VEGETARIAN TAQUITOS

INGREDIENTS

2 poblano chile peppers

2 cups ricotta cheese

Salt, to taste

8 Corn Tortillas (see page 240)

¼ cup extra-virgin olive oil

1 Roast the poblanos over an open flame, on the grill, or in the oven until they are charred all over. Place the poblanos in a bowl, cover the bowl with plastic wrap, and let the poblanos steam for 10 minutes. When cool enough to handle, remove the skins, seeds, and stems from the poblanos and dice the remaining flesh.

2 Stir the poblanos into the ricotta, season the mixture with salt, and set the mixture aside.

3 Place the tortillas in a large, dry cast-iron skillet and warm them for 30 seconds on each side. Fill the tortillas with the cheese-and-poblano mixture and roll them up tight, tucking in the ends of the tortillas in so that the taquitos do not come apart.

4 Place the olive oil in the skillet and warm it over medium heat. Place the tortillas in the pan, seam side down, and cook for 1 minute before turning them over. Cook the taquitos until browned all over, about 5 minutes.

5 Transfer the taquitos to a paper towel–lined plate and let them drain and cool slightly before enjoying.

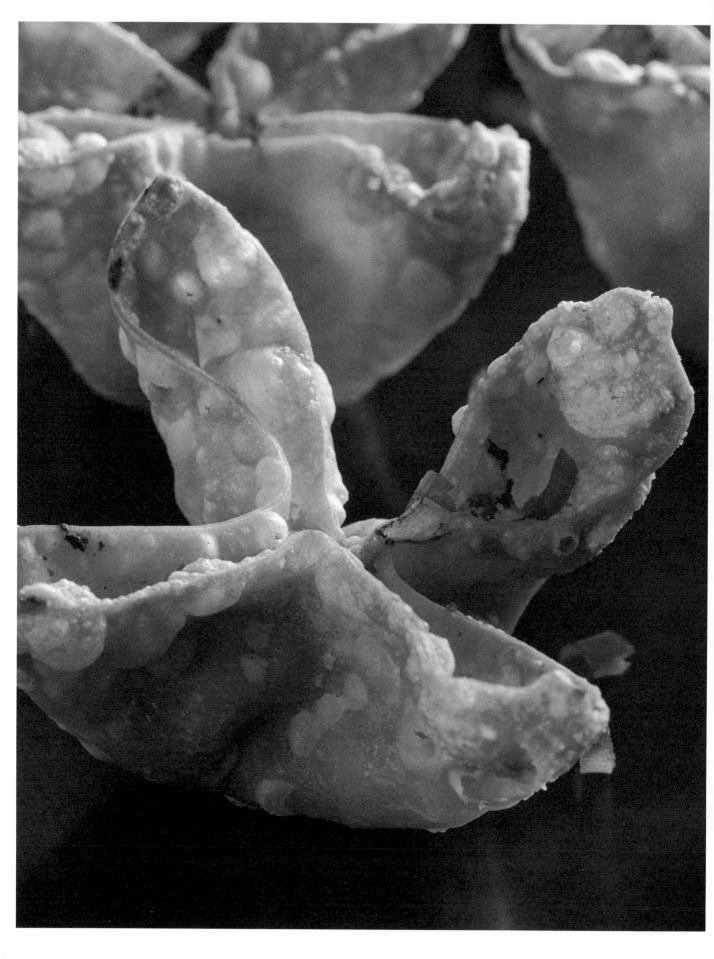

CRAB RANGOON

INGREDIENTS

1 lb. cream cheese, softened

6 oz. fresh crabmeat

2 tablespoons confectioners' sugar

¼ teaspoon kosher salt

40 square Wonton Wrappers (see page 242)

Canola oil, as needed

1   Place the cream cheese, crabmeat, sugar, and salt in a medium bowl and fold the mixture until it is well combined.

2   Place 1 tablespoon of the mixture in the middle of a wrapper. Rub the wrapper's edges with a moist finger, bring the corners together, and pinch to seal tightly. Transfer the dumpling to a parchment paper-lined baking sheet and repeat with the remaining wrappers and filling.

3   Add canola oil to a Dutch oven until it is 2 inches deep and warm it to 325°F over medium heat. Working in batches to avoid crowding the pot, gently slip the dumplings into the hot oil and fry, while turning, until they are golden brown all over, about 3 minutes.

4   Transfer the fried dumplings to a paper towel-lined wire rack and let them drain and cool slightly before enjoying.

ARANCINI

INGREDIENTS

5 cups Chicken Stock
(see page 237)

½ cup unsalted butter

2 cups Arborio rice

1 small white onion, grated

1 cup white wine

4 oz. Fontina cheese, grated,
plus more for garnish

Salt and pepper, to taste

Canola oil, as needed

6 large eggs, beaten

5 cups panko

Marinara Sauce (see page 243),
for serving

1 Bring the stock to a simmer in a large saucepan. In a large skillet, melt the butter over high heat. Add the rice and onion to the skillet and cook until the rice has a toasty fragrance, about 3 minutes. Deglaze the skillet with the white wine and cook until the rice has almost completely absorbed the wine.

2 Reduce the heat to medium-high and begin adding the stock ¼ cup at a time, stirring until it has been absorbed by the rice. Continue adding the stock until the rice is al dente.

3 Turn off the heat, stir in the cheese, and season the risotto with salt and pepper. Pour it onto a rimmed baking sheet and let it cool.

4 Add canola oil to a Dutch oven until it is 2 inches deep and warm it to 350°F. When the risotto is cool, form it into golf ball-sized spheres. Dredge them in the eggs and then the panko until completely coated.

5 Working in batches to avoid crowding the pot, gently slip the arancini into the hot oil and fry until they are warmed through and golden brown, 3 to 5 minutes. Transfer the arancini to a paper towel-lined plate to drain and let them cool slightly.

6 To serve, spoon the Marinara Sauce onto a serving plate, top with the arancini, and garnish with additional Fontina.

STEAMED PORK BUNS

INGREDIENTS

Steamed Buns (see page 244)

1 teaspoon fennel seeds

2 star anise pods

1 cinnamon stick

1 teaspoon peppercorns

6 whole cloves

1 bay leaf

¼ cup kosher salt

1½ lbs. pork belly, fat side scored ¼ inch deep

Pickled vegetables, for topping

1 Start your preparations the night before making the Steamed Buns. Place 6 cups of water, the fennel seeds, star anise pods, cinnamon stick, peppercorns, whole cloves, bay leaf, and salt in a saucepan and bring to a boil. Turn off the heat and let the mixture cool completely. Place the pork belly in a roasting pan and pour the cooled liquid into the pan. Place the pan in the refrigerator overnight.

2 Preheat the oven to 450°F and rinse the pork belly. Place the pork belly on a rimmed baking sheet, scored side up, place it in the oven, and roast for 30 minutes. Lower the temperature to 275°F and roast the pork belly until it is tender, but not mushy, about 1 hour. While the pork belly is roasting, prepare the Steamed Buns.

3 When the pork belly is done, remove it from the oven and let it rest for 20 minutes. Place a few inches of water in a saucepan and bring it to a boil. Place a steaming basket above the water and, working in batches if necessary to avoid crowding the steaming basket, place the buns in the steamer tray, making sure to leave them on the pieces of parchment paper. Steam the buns for 10 minutes.

4 Slice the pork belly thin and fill the buns with it. Top with your favorite pickled vegetables and serve.

CHICKEN 65

INGREDIENTS

1 lb. boneless, skinless chicken thighs, chopped

1 teaspoon mashed fresh ginger

1 garlic clove, minced

½ teaspoon chili powder, plus more to taste

1 teaspoon fresh lemon juice

½ teaspoon black pepper, plus more to taste

⅛ teaspoon turmeric

Salt, to taste

2 tablespoons cornstarch

1 tablespoon rice flour

Canola oil, as needed

½ teaspoon sugar

2 tablespoons plain yogurt

1 tablespoon unsalted butter

3 to 5 curry leaves

2 green chile peppers, stems and seeds removed, chopped

½ teaspoon cumin

1. Rinse the chicken and pat it dry. Place the ginger, one-third of the garlic, the chili powder, lemon juice, black pepper, turmeric, and salt in a mixing bowl and stir to combine. Add the chicken and stir to coat. Place it in the refrigerator and marinate for at least 1 hour.

2. When ready to cook the chicken, place the cornstarch and flour in a mixing bowl, stir to combine, and dredge the marinated chicken in the mixture.

3. Add canola oil to a Dutch oven until it is 2 inches deep and warm it to 350°F over medium heat.

4. Place the sugar, remaining garlic, and yogurt in a mixing bowl, season with chili powder and salt, and stir to combine. Set the mixture aside.

5. Working in batches to avoid crowding the pot, gently slip the chicken into the hot oil and fry until golden brown and cooked through. Remove the fried chicken from the pot and let it drain on a paper towel–lined plate.

6. Place the butter, curry leaves, chiles, and cumin in a small pan and cook over medium heat, stirring frequently, until fragrant. Stir in the yogurt mixture and bring the sauce to a simmer. Add the fried chicken to the sauce and cook until the chicken has absorbed most of the liquid. Let the chicken cool briefly before serving.

SPRING ROLLS

INGREDIENTS

4 oz. pork shoulder, sliced thin

1 tablespoon plus ½ teaspoon cornstarch

2 tablespoons plus ½ teaspoon soy sauce

½ teaspoon rice wine

1¼ teaspoons sesame oil

2 tablespoons oyster sauce

Pinch of five-spice powder

8 dried shiitake mushrooms, soaked, drained, stems removed, finely diced

¼ head of green cabbage, shredded

1 carrot, peeled and grated

2 celery stalks, finely diced

1 cup bean sprouts

3 scallions, trimmed and sliced thin

1½ teaspoons water, plus more as needed

¼ cup all-purpose flour

16 spring roll wrappers

Canola oil, as needed

1 Place the pork, ½ teaspoon of cornstarch, ½ teaspoon of soy sauce, rice wine, and ¼ teaspoon of sesame oil in a bowl and stir until well combined. Let the mixture marinate for 15 minutes.

2 Place the remaining soy sauce, the oyster sauce, five-spice powder, and remaining sesame oil in a separate bowl, stir until combined, and set the mixture aside.

3 Place the pork in a large skillet and stir-fry over medium-high heat until it is nearly cooked through, 4 to 5 minutes. Add the mushrooms, cook for 1 minute, and then stir in the remaining vegetables and cook, stirring frequently, for 3 minutes.

4 Place the remaining cornstarch and the water in a bowl and stir to combine. Stir the slurry and the soy sauce mixture into the pan and cook until the liquid has thickened. Transfer the mixture to a baking sheet and let it cool.

5 Place the flour in a bowl and add enough water until you have a paste. Divide the filling among the spring roll wrappers, roll them up, and seal each one with some of the flour paste. Place the spring rolls on a baking sheet and cover them with plastic wrap.

6 Add canola oil to a Dutch oven until it is about 2 inches deep and warm it to 350°F. Working in batches to avoid crowding the pot, add the spring rolls and fry until they are crispy and golden brown. Transfer the fried spring rolls to a paper towel-lined plate to drain.

7 When all of the spring rolls have been cooked, serve with your favorite dipping sauce.

SPRING ROLLS, SEE PAGE 63

POPCORN CHICKEN

INGREDIENTS

3 garlic cloves, smashed

1 egg white

1 tablespoon soy sauce

1½ tablespoons sesame oil

½ teaspoon white pepper

1 tablespoon cornstarch

Salt, to taste

1 lb. boneless, skin-on chicken breast, cut into bite-sized pieces

7 tablespoons tapioca starch, plus more as needed

2 cups canola oil

1 Place the garlic, egg white, soy sauce, sesame oil, white pepper, cornstarch, and salt in a mixing bowl and stir to combine. Add the chicken, toss to coat, and cover the bowl. Chill in the refrigerator for 1 hour.

2 Dust a baking sheet with the tapioca starch, add the chicken, and turn it in the starch until it is evenly coated, adding more tapioca starch as necessary.

3 Place the canola oil in a Dutch oven and warm it to 350°F. Shake the chicken to remove any excess starch. Working in batches to avoid crowding the pot, gently slip it into the hot oil and fry until it is golden brown and cooked through, 8 to 10 minutes.

4 Place the fried chicken on a paper towel-lined plate to drain and briefly let it cool before serving with your favorite dipping sauce.

YIELD: 24 WONTONS • ACTIVE TIME: 35 MINUTES • TOTAL TIME: 45 MINUTES

PORK & SHRIMP WONTONS

INGREDIENTS

½ lb. ground pork

4 oz. shrimp, shells removed, deveined, minced

1 tablespoon minced shallot

1 tablespoon chopped fresh chives

1 tablespoon fish sauce

2 tablespoons white miso

1 tablespoon shrimp paste

2 tablespoons chopped radish

1 tablespoon toasted sesame seeds

1 teaspoon sesame oil

1 teaspoon sherry

24 square Wonton Wrappers (see page 242)

1 Place the pork in a skillet and cook it over medium heat until it is browned all over and cooked through, about 8 minutes, breaking it up with wooden spoon as it cooks. Remove the pan from heat and let the pork cool completely.

2 Place a bowl of cold water near your work surface. Place the pork and all of the remaining ingredients, except for the Wonton Wrappers, in a mixing bowl and stir until well combined.

3 Place 2 teaspoons of the mixture in the center of a wrapper. Dip your finger into the cold water and rub it around the edges of the wrapper. Bring each corner of the wrapper together and press to seal the wonton. Repeat with the remaining wrappers and filling.

4 Place 2 inches of water in a large saucepan and bring it to a simmer. Place the wontons in a steaming basket, place the basket over the simmering water, and steam the wontons until they are cooked through, about 8 minutes. Remove the wontons from the steaming basket and let them cool slightly before enjoying.

TAKOYAKI

INGREDIENTS

2 teaspoons sake

2 teaspoons mirin

2 teaspoons soy sauce

2 teaspoons oyster sauce

2 teaspoons Worcestershire sauce

1 tablespoon sugar

1 tablespoon ketchup

Salt and white pepper, to taste

2 tablespoons water, plus more as needed

1 large egg

1½ cups Chicken Stock (see page 237)

¾ cup all-purpose flour

1 cup minced cooked octopus

2 scallion greens, sliced thin

¼ cup minced pickled ginger

Okonomiyaki Sauce (see page 245), for serving

1 Place the sake, mirin, soy sauce, oyster sauce, Worcestershire sauce, sugar, ketchup, salt, and white pepper in a mixing bowl and stir to combine. Set the mixture aside.

2 Place the water, egg, and stock in a bowl and stir until combined. Sprinkle the flour over the mixture and stir until all the flour has been incorporated and the mixture comes together as a thick batter. Add the sake-and-mirin mixture and stir to incorporate. Pour the batter into a measuring cup with a spout.

3 Coat the wells of an aebleskiver pan or a muffin pan with nonstick cooking spray and place it over medium heat. When the pan is hot, fill the wells of the pan halfway with the batter and add a pinch of octopus, scallion, and pickled ginger to each. Fill the wells the rest of the way with the batter, until they are almost overflowing.

4 Cook the dumplings for approximately 2 minutes and use a chopstick to flip each one over. Turn the takoyaki as needed until they are golden brown on both sides and piping hot.

5 Transfer the takoyaki to a serving platter, drizzle the sauce over the top, and enjoy.

SPANAKOPITA

INGREDIENTS

½ lb. baby spinach, stems removed

1 cup crumbled feta cheese

6 tablespoons full-fat Greek yogurt

2 scallions, trimmed and chopped

1 egg, beaten

2 tablespoons chopped fresh mint

2 garlic cloves, minced

Zest and juice of ½ lemon

½ teaspoon freshly grated nutmeg

Pinch of cayenne pepper

Salt and pepper, to taste

½ lb. frozen phyllo dough, thawed

6 tablespoons unsalted butter, melted

1 cup freshly grated Pecorino Romano cheese

1 tablespoon sesame seeds

1 tablespoon chopped fresh dill

1   Prepare an ice bath. Fill a large saucepan three-quarters of the way with water and bring it to a boil. Add the spinach and boil for 2 minutes, making sure it is all submerged. Drain the spinach, plunge it in the ice bath, and let it cool.

2   Place the spinach in a linen towel and wring the towel to remove as much water from the spinach as possible. Chop the spinach, place it in a bowl, and add the feta, yogurt, scallions, egg, mint, garlic, lemon zest, lemon juice, nutmeg, and cayenne. Stir to combine, season the mixture with salt and pepper, and set the filling aside.

3   Preheat the oven to 425°F. Line a baking sheet with parchment paper. Place a piece of parchment paper on a work surface, place a sheet of phyllo on it, and brush with some of the butter. Lay another sheet of phyllo on top, gently press down, and brush it with butter. Sprinkle a thin layer of the Pecorino over it. Repeat so that you have another layer of Pecorino sandwiched between two 2-sheet layers of phyllo. Make sure you keep any phyllo you are not working with covered so that it does not dry out.

4   Working from the top of the rectangle, find the center point and cut down, as though you were cutting an open book in half. Cut these halves in two, so that you have four strips. Place 2 tablespoons of the filling on the bottom of each strip and shape the filling into a triangle. Maintaining the triangle shape of the filling, fold the strips up into triangles, as if you were folding a flag. Crimp the pastries to seal and place the spanakopita on the baking sheet, seam side down.

5   Repeat Steps 3 and 4, giving you 8 spanakopita. Sprinkle the sesame seeds over each spanakopita, place them in the oven, and bake until golden brown, about 20 minutes. Remove the spanakopita from the oven, sprinkle the dill over them, and enjoy.

PUNJABI SAMOSAS

1   To begin preparations for the wrappers, place the flour and salt in a mixing bowl and use your hands to combine. Add the olive oil and work the mixture with your hands until it is a coarse meal. Add the water and knead the mixture until a smooth, firm dough forms. If the dough is too dry, incorporate more water, adding 1 tablespoon at a time. Cover the bowl with a kitchen towel and set it aside.

2   To begin preparations for the filling, place the potatoes in a saucepan and cover them with water. Bring the water to a boil and cook until the potatoes are fork-tender, about 20 minutes. Drain the potatoes, place them in a bowl, mash until smooth, and set them aside.

3   Place the olive oil in a skillet and warm it over medium heat. Add the crushed seeds and toast until they are fragrant, about 2 minutes, shaking the pan frequently. Add the ginger, garlic, and jalapeño, stir-fry for 2 minutes, and then add the chili powder, turmeric, amchoor powder, and garam masala.

Cook for another minute before adding the mashed potatoes. Stir to combine, season with salt, and taste the mixture. Adjust the seasoning as necessary, transfer the mixture to a bowl, and let it cool completely.

4   Divide the dough for the wrappers into 8 pieces and roll each one out into a 6-inch circle on a flour-dusted work surface. Cut the circles in half and brush the flat edge of each piece with water. Fold one corner of the flat edge toward the other to make a cone and pinch to seal. Fill each cone one-third of the way with the filling, brush the opening with water, and pinch to seal. Place the sealed samosas on a parchment-lined baking sheet.

5   Add canola oil to a Dutch oven until it is 2 inches deep and warm to 325°F. Working in batches to avoid crowding the pot, add the filled samosas to the hot oil and fry, turning them as they cook, until they are golden brown, about 5 minutes. Transfer the cooked samosas to a paper towel–lined plate to drain and serve once they have all been cooked.

INGREDIENTS

For the Wrappers

2 cups maida flour, plus more as needed

¼ teaspoon kosher salt

2 tablespoons extra-virgin olive oil

½ cup water, plus more as needed

For the Filling

2 russet potatoes, peeled and chopped

2 tablespoons extra-virgin olive oil

1 teaspoon coriander seeds, crushed

½ teaspoon fennel seeds, crushed

Pinch of fenugreek seeds, crushed

1-inch piece of fresh ginger, peeled and grated

1 garlic clove, grated

1 teaspoon minced jalapeño chile pepper

2 teaspoons chili powder

¾ teaspoon turmeric

1 tablespoon amchoor powder

½ teaspoon garam masala

Salt, to taste

Canola oil, as needed

SWEET & SOUR MEATBALLS

INGREDIENTS

2 lbs. ground beef

½ small onion, diced

½ cup bread crumbs

2 eggs

1 teaspoon kosher salt

1 teaspoon black pepper

1½ cups ketchup

¾ cup Concord grape jelly

1 Preheat the oven to 350°F and line a baking sheet with aluminum foil. Place the beef, onion, bread crumbs, eggs, salt, and pepper in a mixing bowl and stir until combined. Working with wet hands, form the mixture into 1-inch meatballs and arrange them on the baking sheet.

2 Place the meatballs in the oven and bake until they are browned all over, 15 to 20 minutes, turning them as necessary.

3 Place the ketchup and jelly in a medium saucepan and warm over medium-low heat, stirring until the jelly has melted. Raise the heat to medium and bring the mixture to a boil.

4 Add the meatballs to the sauce, reduce the heat to low, and simmer the meatballs until they have the desired flavor and are cooked through, 15 to 20 minutes.

FALAFEL

INGREDIENTS

1 (14 oz.) can of chickpeas, drained and rinsed

½ red onion, chopped

1 cup fresh parsley, chopped

1 cup fresh cilantro, chopped

3 bunches of scallions, trimmed and chopped

1 jalapeño chile pepper, stem and seeds removed, chopped

3 garlic cloves

1 teaspoon cumin

1 teaspoon kosher salt, plus more to taste

½ teaspoon cardamom

¼ teaspoon black pepper

2 tablespoons chickpea flour

½ teaspoon baking soda

Canola oil, as needed

Hummus (see page 247), for serving

1 Line a baking sheet with parchment paper. Place all of the ingredients, except for the canola oil and Hummus, in a food processor and puree until smooth.

2 Scoop ¼-cup portions of the puree onto the baking sheet and place it in the refrigerator for 1 hour.

3 Add canola oil to a Dutch oven until it is 2 inches deep and warm it to 320°F over medium heat.

4 Working in batches, add the falafel to the hot oil and fry, turning occasionally, until they are golden brown, about 6 minutes. Transfer the cooked falafel to a paper towel–lined plate to drain.

5 When all of the falafel have been cooked, serve with the Hummus.

FALAFEL, SEE PAGE 77

HUSH PUPPIES

INGREDIENTS

1 cup all-purpose flour

1½ cups cornmeal

2 tablespoons baking powder

2 tablespoons sugar

1 tablespoon baking soda

2 teaspoons kosher salt

½ teaspoon cayenne pepper

1¼ cups buttermilk

2 eggs

1 large yellow onion, grated

Canola oil, as needed

1 Place the flour, cornmeal, baking powder, sugar, baking soda, salt, and cayenne in a large bowl and stir to combine.

2 Place the buttermilk, eggs, and the grated onion (along with any juices that have collected) in a bowl and stir to combine. Add the wet mixture to the dry mixture, stir to combine, and let the batter sit for 1 hour.

3 Add canola oil to a large Dutch oven until it is 2 inches deep and warm to 350°F. Working in batches to avoid crowding the pot, gently drop tablespoons of the batter into the hot oil. Cook, turning the hush puppies as they brown, until they are crispy and golden brown, 3 to 4 minutes. Transfer the hush puppies to a paper towel-lined plate to drain and let them cool slightly before enjoying with your favorite dipping sauce.

QUESO FUNDIDO

INGREDIENTS

6 oz. Oaxaca cheese, cubed

½ plum tomato, diced

¼ white onion, diced

2 tablespoons diced green chile peppers

2 tablespoons sugar

¼ cup fresh lime juice

1 teaspoon chili powder

1 oz. tequila

1　Preheat the oven to 350°F. Place the cheese, tomato, onion, and chiles in a small cast-iron skillet and stir to combine. Set the mixture aside.

2　Combine the sugar, lime juice, and chili powder in a small saucepan and cook over medium heat, stirring to dissolve the sugar, until the mixture is syrupy.

3　Drizzle the syrup over the cheese mixture, place it in the oven, and bake until the cheese has melted and is golden brown on top, about 15 minutes.

4　Remove the pan from the oven, pour the tequila over the mixture, and use a long match or a wand lighter to ignite it. Bring the flaming skillet to the table and enjoy once the flames have gone out.

SOUPS & STEWS

There may be no group of foods that supply the measure of comfort that soups and stews do. Simply put, a bowl filled with a warm, nourishing broth, meat, and/or vegetables is supremely capable of keeping the harsh, cold world from closing in, allowing you to go through your day as though nothing could possibly go wrong.

CHICKEN NOODLE SOUP

INGREDIENTS

1 tablespoon extra-virgin olive oil

½ onion, minced

1 carrot, peeled and diced

1 celery stalk, minced

1 teaspoon fresh thyme

4 cups Chicken Stock
(see page 237)

Salt and pepper, to taste

1½ cups egg noodles

1 cooked chicken breast,
chopped

1   Place the olive oil in a medium saucepan and warm it over medium heat. Add the onion and cook, stirring occasionally, until it starts to soften, about 5 minutes. Add the carrot and celery and cook, stirring occasionally, until they start to soften, about 5 minutes.

2   Add the thyme and stock and bring the soup to a boil. Reduce the heat so that the soup simmers and cook for 20 minutes.

3   Season the soup with salt and pepper, add the egg noodles, and cook until they are al dente, about 7 minutes. Stir in the chicken and simmer for 2 minutes. Ladle the soup into warmed bowls and enjoy.

CREAMY HADDOCK CHOWDER

INGREDIENTS

4 slices of thick-cut bacon

1 large onion, chopped

4 cups cubed potatoes

4 cups Fish Stock (see page 248)

1½ lbs. haddock fillets, skin removed, cut into ½-inch cubes

2 tablespoons chopped fresh parsley

1 tablespoon chopped fresh chives

1 tablespoon chopped fresh tarragon

2 cups heavy cream

Salt and pepper, to taste

Saltines, for serving

1   Place the bacon in a medium saucepan and cook it over medium-low heat until it is crispy, about 10 minutes. Remove the bacon with a slotted spoon and let it drain on a paper towel–lined plate. When cool enough to handle, chop the bacon into bite-sized pieces.

2   Add the onion and potatoes to the saucepan and cook, stirring occasionally, until they start to brown, about 10 minutes.

3   Add the stock and bring the soup to a boil. Reduce the heat so that the soup simmers and cook until the potatoes are fork-tender, about 10 minutes.

4   Add the haddock and fresh herbs and simmer until the haddock is cooked through, about 10 minutes.

5   Stir in the cream and bacon and gently return the soup to a simmer. Season it with salt and pepper, ladle it into warm bowls, and serve with saltines.

AVGOLEMONO

INGREDIENTS

6 cups Chicken Stock
(see page 237)

½ cup orzo

3 eggs

1 tablespoon fresh lemon juice

1½ cups chopped leftover
chicken

Salt and pepper, to taste

Lemon slices, for garnish

Fresh parsley, chopped, for
garnish

1 Place the stock in a large saucepan and bring it to a boil. Reduce the heat so that the stock simmers, add the orzo, and cook until it is tender, about 5 minutes.

2 Strain the stock and orzo over a large bowl. Set the orzo aside. Return the stock to the pan and bring it to a simmer.

3 Place the eggs in a mixing bowl and beat until they are scrambled and frothy. Stir in the lemon juice and 1 tablespoon cold water. While stirring constantly, incorporate approximately ½ cup of the stock into the egg mixture. Stir another cup of stock into the egg mixture and then stir the tempered eggs into the saucepan. Be careful not to let the stock come to boil once you add the tempered eggs.

4 Add the chicken and return the orzo to the soup. Cook, while stirring, until everything is warmed through, about 3 minutes. Season with salt and pepper, ladle the soup into warm bowls, and garnish with the slices of lemon and parsley.

TOFU TOM YAM GUNG

INGREDIENTS

¼ cup extra-virgin olive oil

1 onion, minced

1 garlic clove, minced

6 cups Vegetable Stock (see page 249)

¼ cup fresh lime juice

3 makrut lime leaves

3 chile peppers, stems and seeds removed, sliced

2 tablespoons chopped fresh cilantro

1 lemongrass stalk, bruised

1 tablespoon sugar

¾ lb. extra-firm tofu, drained and chopped

¼ cup soy sauce

8 shiitake mushrooms, stems removed, sliced

Salt and pepper, to taste

Bean sprouts or yu choy, for garnish

1. Place 2 tablespoons of the olive oil in a medium saucepan and warm it over medium heat. Add the onion and garlic and cook, stirring frequently, until the onion starts to soften, about 5 minutes. Add the stock, lime juice, lime leaves, chiles, cilantro, lemongrass stalk, and sugar and bring to a boil.

2. Place the remaining olive oil in a large skillet and warm it over medium heat. Add the tofu and cook, stirring frequently, until it is lightly browned on all sides. Remove the tofu from the pan and set it aside.

3. Strain the broth through a fine sieve, discard the solids, and place the liquid in a clean pan. Add the soy sauce and shiitake mushrooms and bring to a simmer. Add the tofu and cook for another 4 minutes.

4. Season the soup with salt and pepper, ladle it into warm bowls, and garnish with bean sprouts or yu choy.

Tip: If you can't find lemongrass at your grocery store, substitute 1 teaspoon of fresh lemon juice and a pinch of ground ginger.

CINCINNATI CHILI

INGREDIENTS

2 tablespoons extra-virgin olive oil

1 onion, chopped

1½ lbs. ground beef

2 tablespoons chili powder, or to taste

1 teaspoon cinnamon

1 teaspoon cumin

¼ teaspoon allspice

¼ teaspoon ground cloves

2 bay leaves

2 cups Beef Stock (see page 239)

1 cup tomato sauce

2 tablespoons apple cider vinegar

¼ teaspoon cayenne pepper

1 oz. unsweetened chocolate, grated

Salt and pepper, to taste

½ lb. spaghetti, cooked

Cheddar cheese, shredded, for garnish

Fresh parsley, chopped, for garnish

Garlic bread, for serving

1 Place the olive oil in a medium saucepan and warm it over medium heat. Add the onion and cook, stirring frequently, until it starts to soften, about 5 minutes.

2 Add the ground beef and cook, using a wooden spoon to break it up, until it is browned, about 6 minutes.

3 Stir in the chili powder, cinnamon, cumin, allspice, cloves, bay leaves, stock, tomato sauce, vinegar, and cayenne pepper and bring the chili to a boil. Reduce the heat to low, cover the pan, and cook for 1 hour, stirring occasionally.

4 Remove the pot from heat, stir in the chocolate, and season with salt and pepper. Place a bed of spaghetti in each of the serving bowls. Pour the chili on top, garnish with cheddar cheese and parsley, and serve with garlic bread.

BOUILLABAISSE

INGREDIENTS

6 tablespoons extra-virgin olive oil

1 onion, chopped

1 cup chopped leeks

½ cup sliced celery

1 cup chopped fennel

2 garlic cloves, minced

Bouquet Garni (see page 250)

Zest of 1 orange

1 tomato, peeled, deseeded, and chopped

Pinch of saffron

6 cups Fish Stock (see page 248)

2 teaspoons Pernod

1 tablespoon tomato paste

1 lb. monkfish, cut into 1-inch cubes

12 small shrimp, shells removed, deveined

12 steamer clams

24 mussels

Salt and pepper, to taste

Fresh parsley, chopped, for garnish

Crusty bread, toasted, for serving

1 Place ¼ cup of the olive oil in a large saucepan and warm it over medium heat. Add the onion, leeks, celery, and fennel and cook, stirring occasionally, until the vegetables have softened, about 10 minutes.

2 Add the garlic, Bouquet Garni, orange zest, and tomato and cook, stirring continually, for 1 minute. Stir in the saffron, stock, Pernod, and tomato paste and bring the soup to a boil. Reduce the heat and simmer the soup for 20 minutes.

3 While the soup is simmering, place the remaining olive oil in a skillet and warm it over medium heat. Add the monkfish and shrimp and cook for 2 minutes on each side. Remove the shrimp and monkfish from the pan and set them aside.

4 Add the clams to the soup and cook for 3 minutes. Add the mussels and cook until the majority of the clams and mussels have opened, 3 to 4 minutes. Discard any clams and mussels that do not open.

5 Add the monkfish and shrimp to the soup and cook until warmed through.

6 Season the soup with salt and pepper and ladle it into warmed bowls. Garnish each portion with parsley and serve with crusty bread.

SPLIT PEA SOUP WITH SMOKED HAM

INGREDIENTS

2 tablespoons unsalted butter

1 onion, minced

1 carrot, peeled and minced

1 celery stalk, minced

5 cups Chicken Stock
(see page 237)

1 cup yellow split peas

½ lb. smoked ham, chopped

2 tablespoons finely chopped
fresh parsley, plus more for
garnish

1 bay leaf

1 teaspoon fresh thyme

Salt and pepper, to taste

Lemon wedges, for serving

1   Place the butter in a large saucepan and melt over medium heat. Add the onion, carrot, and celery and cook, stirring frequently, until they have softened, about 5 minutes.

2   Add the stock, split peas, ham, parsley, bay leaf, and thyme. Bring the soup to a boil, reduce the heat to medium-low, and simmer, stirring occasionally, until the peas are al dente, about 1 hour.

3   Remove the bay leaf and discard it. Season the soup with salt and pepper and ladle it into warmed bowls. Garnish with additional parsley and serve with lemon wedges.

ROMESCO DE PEIX

INGREDIENTS

½ cup slivered almonds

½ teaspoon saffron

¼ cup boiling water

½ cup extra-virgin olive oil

1 large yellow onion, chopped

2 large red bell peppers, stems and seeds removed, chopped

2½ teaspoons sweet paprika

1 tablespoon smoked paprika

1 bay leaf

2 tablespoons tomato paste

½ cup sherry

2 cups Fish Stock (see page 248)

1 (28 oz.) can of chopped tomatoes, with their liquid

Salt and pepper, to taste

1½ lbs. monkfish fillets, cut into large pieces

1 lb. mussels, rinsed well and debearded

Fresh cilantro, finely chopped, for garnish

1   Place the almonds in a large cast-iron skillet and toast them over medium heat until they are just browned. Transfer them to a food processor and pulse until they are finely ground.

2   Place the saffron and boiling water in a bowl and let the mixture steep.

3   Place the olive oil in a Dutch oven and warm over medium heat. Add the onion and bell peppers and cook, stirring occasionally, until the peppers are tender, about 15 minutes.

4   Add the sweet paprika, smoked paprika, bay leaf, and tomato paste and cook, stirring constantly, for 1 minute. Add the sherry and bring the mixture to a boil. Boil for 5 minutes and then stir in the stock, tomatoes, saffron, and the soaking liquid. Stir to combine, season with salt and pepper, and reduce the heat so that the soup simmers.

5   Stir in the ground almonds and cook until the mixture thickens slightly, about 8 minutes. Add the fish and mussels, stir gently to incorporate, and simmer until the fish is cooked through and a majority of the mussels have opened, about 5 minutes. Discard any mussels that do not open.

6   Ladle the mixture into warmed bowls, garnish with cilantro, and enjoy.

CORN CHOWDER

INGREDIENTS

Kernels from 6 ears of corn, cobs reserved

6 slices of bacon, chopped

1 large white onion, chopped

2 large potatoes, peeled and chopped

3 garlic cloves, minced

4 cups heavy cream

Salt and pepper, to taste

1 Place the reserved corn cobs in a large stockpot and cover them with water. Bring to a boil, reduce the heat so that the stock simmers, and cook for 1 hour. Strain the stock, measure out 4 cups, and reserve it.

2 Place the bacon in a medium saucepan and cook over low heat until the fat has rendered. Add the onion, raise the heat to medium, and cook, stirring frequently, until the onion starts to soften, about 5 minutes.

3 Add the potatoes and corn kernels and cook, stirring occasionally, for another 10 minutes. Stir in the garlic and the reserved stock and cook, stirring occasionally, until the liquid has reduced by one-third.

4 Add the cream, reduce the heat, and gently simmer the soup for 30 minutes.

5 Season the soup with salt and pepper, ladle it into warm bowls, and enjoy.

HARIRA

INGREDIENTS

3 tablespoons unsalted butter

1½ lbs. boneless, skinless chicken thighs

Salt and pepper, to taste

1 large onion, finely diced

5 garlic cloves, minced

1-inch piece of fresh ginger, peeled and grated

2 teaspoons turmeric

1 teaspoon cumin

½ teaspoon cinnamon

⅛ teaspoon cayenne pepper

¾ cup finely chopped fresh cilantro

½ cup finely chopped fresh parsley

4 cups Chicken Stock (see page 237)

4 cups water

1 (14 oz.) can of chickpeas, drained and rinsed

1 cup brown lentils, picked over and rinsed

1 (28 oz.) can of crushed tomatoes

½ cup vermicelli broken into 2-inch pieces

2 tablespoons fresh lemon juice, plus more to taste

1 Place the butter in a Dutch oven and melt it over medium-high heat. Season the chicken thighs with salt and pepper, place them in the pot, and cook until browned on both sides, about 8 minutes. Remove the chicken from the pot and set it on a plate.

2 Add the onion and cook, stirring occasionally, until it starts to brown, about 8 minutes. Add the garlic and ginger and cook until fragrant, about 1 minute. Stir in the turmeric, cumin, cinnamon, and cayenne pepper and cook for 1 minute. Add ½ cup of the cilantro and ¼ cup of the parsley and cook for 1 minute.

3 Stir in the stock, water, chickpeas, and lentils and bring the soup to a simmer. Return the chicken to the pot, reduce the heat to medium-low, partially cover the Dutch oven, and gently simmer, stirring occasionally, until the lentils are just tender, about 20 minutes.

4 Add the tomatoes and vermicelli and simmer, stirring occasionally, until the pasta is tender, about 10 minutes.

5 Stir in the lemon juice and the remaining cilantro and parsley. Taste, adjust the seasoning as necessary, and enjoy.

FRENCH ONION SOUP

INGREDIENTS

3 tablespoons unsalted butter

7 large sweet onions, sliced

2 teaspoons kosher salt

⅓ cup orange juice

3 oz. sherry

2 tablespoons fresh thyme

7 cups Beef Stock (see page 239)

3 garlic cloves, minced

2 teaspoons black pepper

6 slices of day-old bread

1 cup shredded Gruyère cheese

1 cup shredded Emmental cheese

1   Place the butter, onions, and salt in a Dutch oven and cook the mixture over low heat, stirring occasionally, until the onions are dark brown and caramelized, 40 minutes to 1 hour.

2   Deglaze the pot with the orange juice and sherry, using a wooden spoon to scrape any browned bits from the bottom of the pot. Add the thyme, stock, garlic, and pepper, raise the heat to medium, and bring to a simmer. Simmer for 1 hour.

3   While the soup is simmering, preheat the oven to 450°F.

4   After 1 hour, ladle the soup into oven-safe crocks or bowls and place a slice of bread on top of each portion. Sprinkle the cheeses over each portion, place the crocks in the oven, and bake until the cheese begins to brown, about 10 minutes.

5   Carefully remove the bowls from the oven and let the soup cool for 10 minutes before serving.

ALBONDIGAS SOUP

INGREDIENTS

2 lbs. ground beef

1 egg

2 tablespoons cooked white rice

1 tablespoon chopped fresh hierbabuena, plus more to taste

1 teaspoon chopped fresh oregano

½ bunch of fresh parsley, finely chopped

Salt, to taste

4 large tomatoes

¼ onion

2 garlic cloves

1 teaspoon cumin

½ teaspoon tomato paste

2 tablespoons extra-virgin olive oil

3 carrots, peeled and sliced

3 zucchini, sliced

Corn Tortillas (see page 240), warm, for serving

Roasted serrano or jalapeño chile peppers, for serving

1. Place the ground beef, egg, rice, hierbabuena, oregano, and parsley in a bowl, stir until thoroughly combined, and season the mixture with salt. Form the mixture into meatballs that weigh about 1 oz. each.

2. Place the tomatoes, onion, and garlic in a small saucepan, add water to cover, and boil until the vegetables are tender. Drain, add the vegetables to a blender with the cumin and tomato paste, and puree until smooth.

3. Place the olive oil in a large saucepan and warm it over medium heat. Add the puree and cook for 2 minutes.

4. Add 4 cups of water and season with salt. If desired, add more sprigs of hierbabuena to the broth. Bring the broth to a simmer.

5. Add the carrots and meatballs and cook over low heat until the meatballs are completely cooked through, about 20 minutes.

6. Add the zucchini and cook until it is tender, about 5 minutes.

7. Ladle the soup into warmed bowls, serve with warm tortillas and roasted chiles, and enjoy.

LAMB & CANNELLINI SOUP

INGREDIENTS

2 tablespoons extra-virgin olive oil

1 onion, chopped

2 garlic cloves, minced

1½ lbs. ground lamb

3 carrots, peeled and chopped

3 celery stalks, chopped

1 (14 oz.) can of stewed tomatoes, drained

¼ cup finely chopped fresh parsley

2 tablespoons finely chopped fresh thyme

½ lb. dried cannellini beans, soaked overnight and drained

6 cups Chicken Stock (see page 237)

½ lb. baby spinach

¼ cup sliced Kalamata olives

Salt and pepper, to taste

Feta cheese, crumbled, for garnish

1   Place the olive oil in a large saucepan and warm over medium heat. Add the onion and cook, stirring frequently, until it starts to soften, about 5 minutes. Stir in the garlic, cook for 2 minutes, and then add the lamb. Cook until it starts to brown, about 5 minutes, and add the carrots and celery.

2   Cook for 5 minutes, stir in the tomatoes, herbs, cannellini beans, and stock and bring the soup to a boil. Reduce the heat to medium-low, cover the pan, and simmer for 1 hour, until the beans are tender.

3   Add the spinach and olives and cook until the spinach wilts, about 2 minutes. Season the soup with salt and pepper, ladle it into warmed bowls, and garnish each portion with feta cheese.

POTJIEKOS

INGREDIENTS

¼ cup extra-virgin olive oil

4 large yellow onions, chopped

4 teaspoons curry powder

Zest and juice of 1 orange

2 red chile peppers, stems and seeds removed, chopped

4 curry leaves

4 bay leaves

2 lbs. boneless leg of lamb, cubed

1 large white yam, peeled and chopped

1 large sweet potato, peeled and chopped

2 large potatoes, peeled and chopped

4 large carrots, peeled and chopped

4 oz. mushrooms, sliced

4 large garlic cloves

2 cups fresh spinach, stemmed

Salt, to taste

1 Preheat the oven to 300°F. Place the olive oil in a Dutch oven and warm it over medium heat. Add the onions and cook, stirring occasionally, until they are lightly browned, about 5 minutes.

2 Add the curry powder, orange zest, chiles, curry leaves, bay leaves, and lamb and cook, stirring occasionally, until the lamb is browned all over, about 10 minutes.

3 Add the orange juice and enough water to cover the contents of the pot. Layer the yam, sweet potato, potatoes, carrots, mushrooms, and garlic on top. Cover the Dutch oven and place it in the oven. Let the stew cook until the lamb is very tender, 2 to 3 hours.

4 Remove the Dutch oven from the oven, stir in the spinach, and season the stew with salt. Ladle the stew into warmed bowls and enjoy.

LAMB SHARBA

INGREDIENTS

2 tablespoons extra-virgin olive oil

¾ lb. boneless leg of lamb, cut into 1-inch cubes

1 onion, chopped

1 tomato, quartered, deseeded, sliced thin

1 garlic clove, minced

1 tablespoon tomato paste

1 bunch of fresh mint, tied with twine, plus more for garnish

2 cinnamon sticks

1¼ teaspoons turmeric

1¼ teaspoons paprika

½ teaspoons cumin

8 cups Chicken Stock (see page 237)

1 (14 oz.) can of chickpeas, drained and rinsed

¾ cup orzo

Salt and pepper, to taste

1 Place half of the olive oil in a Dutch oven and warm it over medium-high heat. Add the lamb and cook, turning it as necessary, until it is browned all over, about 5 minutes. Remove the lamb with a slotted spoon and place it on a paper towel–lined plate.

2 Add the onion to the pot and cook, stirring occasionally, until it starts to soften, about 5 minutes. Add the tomato, garlic, tomato paste, mint, cinnamon sticks, turmeric, paprika, and cumin and cook, stirring continually, for 1 minute.

3 Add the stock and bring the mixture to a boil. Return the seared lamb to the pot, reduce the heat, and simmer until the lamb is tender, about 30 minutes.

4 Add the chickpeas and orzo and cook until the orzo is tender, about 10 minutes.

5 Remove the mint and discard it. Season the soup with salt and pepper and ladle it into warmed bowls. Garnish with additional mint and enjoy.

YIELD: 4 SERVINGS • ACTIVE TIME: 15 MINUTES • TOTAL TIME: 1 HOUR AND 15 MINUTES

COQ AU VIN

INGREDIENTS

½ lb. thick-cut bacon

4 lb. whole capon or chicken, broken down

Salt and pepper, to taste

1 lb. button mushrooms, chopped

½ lb. pearl onions

2 celery stalks, finely diced

2 carrots, peeled and finely diced

5 sprigs of fresh thyme

1 head of garlic, halved at the equator

½ cup Cognac

¼ cup tomato paste

2 cups red wine

6 cups Chicken Stock (see page 237)

1 Place the bacon in a Dutch oven and cook it over medium heat until it is crispy, about 8 minutes, turning it as necessary. Transfer the bacon to a paper towel-lined plate to drain and cool. When the bacon is cool enough to handle, chop it into bite-size pieces.

2 Season the capon with salt and pepper. Working in batches to avoid crowding the pot, add the capon to the Dutch oven and sear it until it is golden brown on both sides, turning it as necessary. Remove the capon from the pot and set it aside.

3 Add the mushrooms to the pot, raise the heat to high, and cook, stirring once or twice, until they are browned, about 8 minutes.

4 Add the onions, celery, carrots, and thyme and cook, stirring occasionally, until the vegetables have softened, about 8 minutes.

5 Remove the pan from heat, add the garlic and Cognac, and use a long match or a wand lighter to ignite the Cognac. Place the pot over medium heat and cook until the flames go out.

6 Add the tomato paste and cook, stirring continually, for 2 minutes.

7 Deglaze the pot with the red wine, scraping up any browned bits from the bottom. Cook until the wine has reduced by half.

8 Return the capon to the pot, laying it on top of the vegetables. Return the bacon to the pot, add the stock, and bring the dish to a boil. Reduce the heat so that it simmers, cover the pot, and cook until the capon is very tender, about 1 hour.

9 Remove the capon from the pan and set it aside. Raise the heat to high, cook until the liquid in the Dutch oven has reduced by half, and serve.

LOBSTER CIOPPINO

1 Place 3 inches of water in a Dutch oven and bring to a boil. Place the lobster, headfirst, in the pot, cover the pot, and cook until the shell is bright red, about 6 minutes. Remove the lobster from the pot and set aside. Discard the cooking liquid and return the Dutch oven to the stove.

2 Add 2 cups of water to the pot and bring it to a boil. Add the mussels and clams, cover the pot, and cook until the majority of the mussels and clams have opened, about 5 minutes. Drain the mussels and clams, reserving the liquid. Discard any mussels and/or clams that did not open.

3 Place the Dutch oven over medium-high heat and add the olive oil. When the oil is warm, add the fennel and cook, stirring occasionally, until the fennel has softened, about 5 minutes.

4 Add the shallots and cook, stirring occasionally, until they have softened, about 5 minutes.

5 Add the garlic and tomato paste and cook, stirring continually, for 1 minute. Deglaze the pot with the red wine, scraping up any browned bits from the bottom of the pot. Cook until the wine has almost evaporated, about 5 minutes.

6 Add the tomatoes, white wine, stock, bay leaves, red pepper flakes, and a pinch of salt and pepper. Reduce the heat to medium-low, cover the pot, and cook for 30 minutes.

7 While the stew is cooking, remove the meat from the tail and claws of the lobster. Set it aside.

8 Remove the legs from the lobster and add the remaining carcass to the pot. Uncover the pot and cook the stew for 20 minutes.

9 Add the halibut to the pot and cook until it is cooked through, about 5 minutes. Add the lobster meat, clams, mussels, and reserved cooking liquid and cook for 2 minutes.

10 Ladle the stew into warmed bowls and serve with crusty bread.

INGREDIENTS

1¼ lb. lobster

1 lb. P.E.I. mussels, rinsed well and debearded

12 littleneck clams, rinsed well and scrubbed

2 tablespoons extra-virgin olive oil

½ large fennel bulb, trimmed and sliced thin

2 shallots, minced

3 garlic cloves, minced

1 (6 oz.) can of tomato paste

1 cup red wine

1 (28 oz.) can of whole tomatoes, with their liquid, lightly crushed by hand

1 cup white wine

2 cups Fish Stock (see page 248)

2 bay leaves

1 teaspoon red pepper flakes

Salt and pepper, to taste

1 lb. halibut fillets, skin removed, cubed

Crusty bread, for serving

BIRRIA

1 Place the beef in a baking dish and set it aside.

2 Place the guajillo peppers in a dry skillet and toast them over medium heat until they darken and become fragrant and pliable. Submerge them in a bowl of boiling water and let them soak for 15 minutes.

3 Place the peppercorns and cinnamon stick in the skillet and toast until fragrant, shaking the pan frequently. Combine the toasted spices with the oregano, allspice, and cumin and grind the mixture into a fine powder with a mortar and pestle or a spice grinder.

4 Season the meat with salt and the spice powder. Drain the guajillo peppers and place them in a blender along with the garlic and vinegar. Puree until smooth and then rub the puree over the meat until it is coated. Marinate in the refrigerator overnight.

5 Remove the meat from the refrigerator an hour before you intend to cook.

6 Preheat the oven to 350°F. In a large Dutch oven, warm the olive oil over medium heat, add the onion, and cook until translucent, about 3 minutes.

7 Stir in the tomatoes, bay leaves, meat, marinade, and 1 cup of water and bring to a boil. Cover the pot, place it in the oven, and braise until the meat is very tender, about 3 hours.

8 Check the meat every hour to make sure it has enough liquid. You don't want to skim off any of the fat, as this will remove liquid from the pot and flavor from the finished broth.

9 Remove the meat from the pot and shred the pieces that haven't fallen apart. Stir the meat back into the liquid.

10 When serving birria, it is customary to serve a cup of the strained broth as an appetizer with warm tortillas. The stew can also be served with tortillas, the cilantro, and pickled onions.

INGREDIENTS

5 lbs. beef chuck, cut into 3-inch cubes

10 guajillo chile peppers

1 teaspoon black peppercorns

½ cinnamon stick

1 tablespoon dried oregano

1 teaspoon allspice

½ teaspoon cumin

Salt, to taste

5 garlic cloves

2 tablespoons white vinegar

2 tablespoons extra-virgin olive oil

1 onion, finely diced

3 large tomatoes, diced

2 bay leaves

Corn Tortillas (see page 240), warm, for serving

1 bunch of fresh cilantro, chopped, for serving

Pickled Red Onions (see page 251), for serving

PORK BELLY RAMEN

INGREDIENTS

1 lb. skin-on pork belly

½ cup dark soy sauce

¼ cup rice vinegar

4 star anise pods

1 lb. ramen noodles

4 eggs, uncracked

1 bunch of scallions, trimmed and chopped, for garnish

5 sheets of nori, shredded, for garnish

2 tablespoons toasted sesame seeds, for garnish

Hard-boiled eggs, halved, for garnish

1 Preheat the oven to 350°F. Place the pork belly, soy sauce, vinegar, and star anise in a Dutch oven, stir to combine, and bring it to a simmer over medium heat.

2 Cover the Dutch oven and place it in the oven. Braise the pork belly until it is extremely tender, about 3 hours.

3 Remove the pork belly from the oven, cut it into ¼-inch-thick slices, and set it aside.

4 Bring a small saucepan of water to a boil. Place the Dutch oven over medium-high heat and bring the broth to a boil. Add the noodles to the broth and boil until they are tender, about 6 minutes. Divide the noodles and broth among the serving bowls.

5 Add the eggs to the boiling water and cook until the insides are just set, about 5 minutes.

6 Top each serving of noodles with some pork belly. Peel the hard-boiled eggs, cut them in half, and arrange them on top of each portion.

7 Garnish each portion with the scallions, nori, sesame seeds, and hard-boiled eggs and enjoy.

GUMBO

INGREDIENTS

½ cup extra-virgin olive oil

½ lb. andouille sausage, diced

½ lb. boneless, skinless chicken breast, chopped

Salt, to taste

1 yellow onion, finely diced

2 celery stalks, finely diced

1 green bell pepper, stem and seeds removed, finely diced

½ teaspoon cayenne pepper

½ teaspoon dried oregano

½ teaspoon paprika

½ teaspoon dried thyme

½ teaspoon dried basil

½ teaspoon filé powder

1 cup all-purpose flour

5 cups Chicken Stock (see page 237)

2 bay leaves

1 cup diced tomatoes

½ lb. okra, trimmed and chopped

1 lb. shrimp, shells removed, deveined

Rice pilaf, for serving

Scallion greens, chopped, for garnish

1. Place the olive oil in a large saucepan and warm it over medium heat. Add the sausage and cook until it is browned all over, turning it as necessary. Remove the sausage from the pan and set it aside.

2. Season the chicken with salt, add it to the pan, and cook until it is browned all over, turning it as necessary. Remove the chicken from the pan and set it aside.

3. Add the onion, celery, and bell pepper and cook, stirring occasionally, until the onion is translucent, about 3 minutes. Stir in the cayenne, oregano, paprika, thyme, basil, and filé powder and cook for 1 minute.

4. Add the flour and cook, stirring continually, until it is a deep brown and gives off a nutty aroma.

5. Add the stock, bay leaves, and tomatoes and bring the gumbo to a simmer. Return the sausage and chicken to the pan, add the okra, and simmer the gumbo until it has thickened, about 20 minutes.

6. Season the gumbo with salt, add the shrimp, and cook until they turn pink, 4 to 5 minutes.

7. Ladle the gumbo over rice pilaf, garnish with scallion greens, and serve.

ENTREES

When one thinks of comfort food, chances are that one of the preparations contained in this chapter is what immediately comes to mind. Whether it be the simple perfection of a slice of pizza or a platter of tacos, the cozy nostalgia of a grilled cheese, the sublime crunch of fried chicken, or the satisfying substance of a well-made burger, a solution to every single quest for comfort is collected here.

KEFTA

INGREDIENTS

1½ lbs. ground lamb

½ lb. ground beef

½ white onion, minced

2 garlic cloves, roasted and mashed

Zest of 1 lemon

1 cup fresh parsley, chopped

2 tablespoons chopped fresh mint

1 teaspoon cinnamon

2 tablespoons cumin

1 tablespoon paprika

1 teaspoon coriander

Salt and pepper, to taste

¼ cup extra-virgin olive oil

1   Place all the ingredients, except for the olive oil, in a mixing bowl and stir until well combined. Place a small bit of the mixture in a skillet and cook over medium heat until cooked through. Taste and adjust the seasoning in the remaining mixture as necessary. Working with wet hands, form the mixture into 18 ovals and thread them onto six skewers.

2   Place the olive oil in a Dutch oven and warm it over medium-high heat. Working in batches, add three skewers to the pot and sear the kefta until browned all over and nearly cooked through. Transfer the browned kefta to a paper towel–lined plate to drain.

3   When all the kefta have been browned, return the skewers to the pot, cover it, and remove it from heat. Let stand for 10 minutes so the kefta get cooked through.

4   When the kefta are cooked through, remove them from the skewers and enjoy.

TACOS

INGREDIENTS

1 tablespoon extra-virgin olive oil, plus more as needed

1 lb. ground beef

1 tablespoon kosher salt

2 teaspoons cumin

2 teaspoons paprika

1 tablespoon garlic powder

1 teaspoon cayenne pepper

1 teaspoon chili powder

Corn Tortillas (see page 240), for serving

1 Place the olive oil in a large skillet and warm it over medium-high heat.

2 Add the ground beef and all of the seasonings. Cook, breaking up the meat with a wooden spoon, until it is browned and cooked through, about 8 minutes.

3 Serve with the Corn Tortillas and your favorite taco fixings.

TACOS, SEE PAGE 129

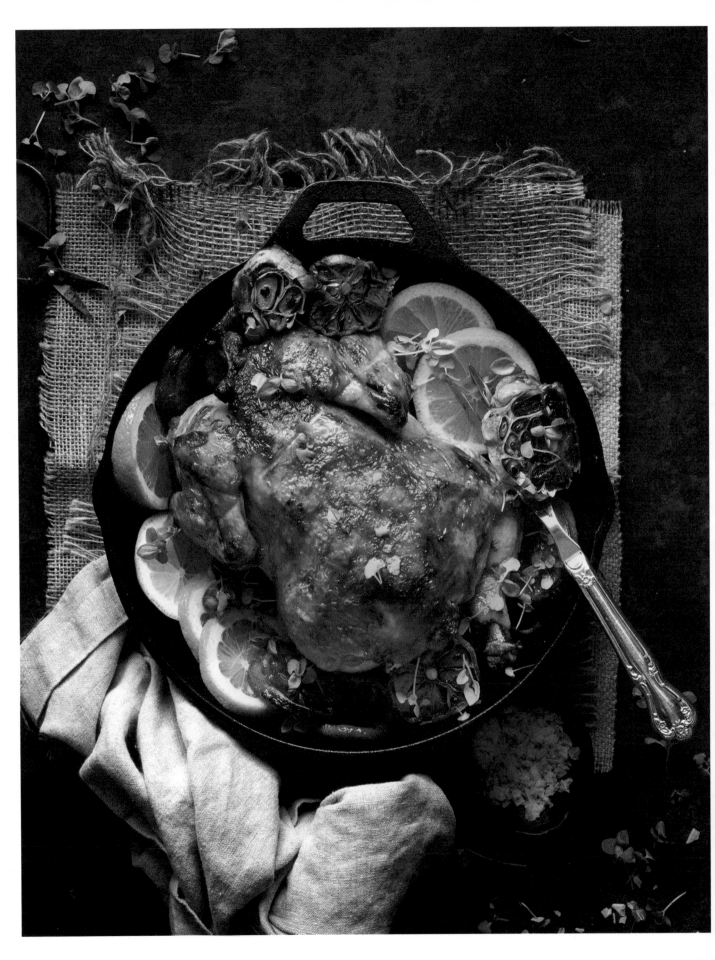

ROASTED CHICKEN

INGREDIENTS

5 lb. whole chicken

Salt and pepper, to taste

2 tablespoons extra-virgin olive oil

1 tablespoon finely chopped fresh thyme

2 lemons, sliced

2 heads of garlic, halved at their equators

1 Place the chicken on a wire rack resting in a baking sheet and pat as dry as possible. Season it generously with salt and pepper and let it chill, uncovered, in the refrigerator overnight.

2 Preheat the oven to 500°F and place a Dutch oven in the oven to warm. Rub the chicken with the olive oil, sprinkle the thyme leaves over the chicken, and stuff the lemon and garlic in its cavity.

3 Carefully remove the Dutch oven from the oven and place the chicken in it, breast side down. Place the chicken in the oven and roast it for 15 minutes.

4 Reduce the oven's temperature to 375°F and continue roasting the chicken until the juices run clear and the internal temperature in the thickest part of the thigh is 165°F, about 35 minutes.

5 Remove the chicken from the oven, transfer it to a wire rack, and let it rest for 15 to 20 minutes before carving.

STEAK FRITES

INGREDIENTS

2 russet potatoes, cut into long, thin fries

Canola oil, as needed

1 lb. rib eye steak

1 tablespoon kosher salt

½ teaspoon black pepper

4 tablespoons unsalted butter

2 garlic cloves

3 sprigs of fresh thyme

1   Place the potatoes in a large container and cover them with water. Let the potatoes soak for 30 minutes.

2   Drain the potatoes, pat them dry, and set them aside.

3   Add canola oil to a Dutch oven until it is about 2 inches deep and warm it to 350°F.

4   While the oil is warming, warm a cast-iron skillet over high heat. Season the steak with the salt and pepper and sear it in the dry skillet for 4 to 6 minutes on each side.

5   Add the butter, garlic, and thyme to the pan and continue to cook the steak, basting it continually, until it is medium-rare (the interior registers 130°F on an instant-read thermometer). Remove the pan from heat and let the steak rest for 10 minutes.

6   Gently slip the potatoes into the hot oil and fry until they are golden brown, about 5 minutes.

7   Transfer the fries to a paper towel-lined plate to drain and season them with salt. Slice the steak and serve alongside the fries.

BEEF & BROCCOLI STIR-FRY

INGREDIENTS

2 garlic cloves

1 tablespoon grated fresh ginger

1 bunch of scallions, trimmed

1 teaspoon red pepper flakes

½ cup extra-virgin olive oil

1 teaspoon sesame oil

1 lb. beef chuck, sliced thin

½ teaspoon kosher salt

1 lb. Chinese broccoli, cut into 2-inch pieces

½ red onion, diced

½ lb. shiitake mushrooms, sliced

1 red bell pepper, stem and seeds removed, finely diced

1 Chinese eggplant, finely diced

1 tablespoon fish sauce

White rice, cooked, for serving

1 Place the garlic, ginger, scallions, and red pepper flakes in a food processor and blitz until smooth. With the food processor running, add the olive oil in a slow stream until it has emulsified. Set the emulsion aside.

2 Place the sesame oil in a large skillet and warm it over medium-high heat. Add the beef, season it with the salt, and cook until the beef is browned all over, about 5 minutes, turning it as needed.

3 Add the broccoli, onion, mushrooms, pepper, eggplant, and emulsion, reduce the heat to medium, and cook, stirring occasionally, until the vegetables are tender and the flavor has developed to your liking, about 10 minutes.

4 Stir in the fish sauce and cook for 1 minute. Serve over rice and enjoy.

GRILLED CHEESE

INGREDIENTS

2 oz. cheddar cheese, grated

2 oz. Gruyère cheese, grated

4 slices of bread (½ inch thick)

2 tablespoons unsalted butter

1   Place the cheeses in a bowl and stir to combine.

2   Divide the cheese mixture between two slices of the bread. Top with the remaining slices of bread and press down gently.

3   Place 1 tablespoon of the butter in a large skillet and melt it over medium heat. Add the sandwiches to the pan and cook until the bottoms turn golden brown, 3 to 4 minutes, reducing the heat if necessary to keep the bread from burning.

4   Add the remaining butter, flip the sandwiches over, press down on them, and cook until the cheese is completely melted and both sides of the sandwiches are golden brown, about 4 minutes. Enjoy immediately.

SPAGHETTI ALLA CARBONARA

INGREDIENTS

2½ tablespoons extra-virgin olive oil

4 oz. pancetta or bacon, diced

Salt and pepper, to taste

2 large eggs, at room temperature

¾ cup freshly grated Parmesan cheese, plus more for garnish

1 lb. spaghetti

1 Bring a large saucepan of water to a boil. Add 2 tablespoons of the olive oil to a large skillet and warm it over medium heat. Add the pancetta and season it with pepper. Cook the pancetta, stirring occasionally, until its fat renders and the meat starts turning golden brown, about 5 minutes. Remove the skillet from heat and cover it partially.

2 Place the eggs in a small bowl and whisk until scrambled. Add the Parmesan, season with salt and pepper, and stir until combined. Set the mixture aside.

3 Add salt and the pasta to the boiling water. Cook 2 minutes short of the directed cooking time, reserve ¼ cup of the pasta water, and drain the pasta.

4 Return the pan to the stove, raise the heat to high, and add the remaining olive oil and the reserved pasta water. Add the drained pasta and toss to combine. Cook until the pasta has absorbed the water.

5 Remove the pot from heat, add the pancetta and the egg-and-Parmesan mixture, and toss to coat the pasta. Divide the pasta between the serving bowls, season with pepper, and top each portion with additional Parmesan.

BEEF STROGANOFF

INGREDIENTS

¼ cup extra-virgin olive oil

2 lbs. beef chuck, cut into 3-inch pieces

Salt, to taste

1½ teaspoons black pepper

1 yellow onion, finely diced

8 garlic cloves, minced

3 sprigs of fresh thyme

2 cups Beef Stock (see page 239)

10 oz. egg noodles

½ cup tomato paste

1 cup sour cream

Fresh parsley, chopped, for garnish

1 Place the olive oil in a Dutch oven and warm it over medium-high heat. Season the beef with salt and the pepper, add it to the pot, and cook until it is browned all over, about 10 minutes, turning it as necessary.

2 Add the onion and cook, stirring occasionally, until it is translucent, about 3 minutes.

3 Add the garlic, thyme, and stock, bring to a simmer, and reduce the heat so that the stroganoff simmers gently. Cook until the beef is very tender, about 1 hour and 30 minutes.

4 While the stroganoff is simmering, bring water to a boil in a large saucepan. Add salt and the egg noodles and cook until the noodles are al dente, about 8 minutes. Drain the noodles and set them aside.

5 Remove the beef from the pot and raise the heat. Cook until the liquid in the pot has reduced by half, about 15 minutes.

6 Stir in the tomato paste and sour cream, add the egg noodles, and return the beef to the pot. Cook, stirring continually, until everything is warmed through.

7 Ladle the stroganoff into warmed bowls, garnish each portion with parsley, and enjoy.

PULLED PORK

INGREDIENTS

6 lbs. pork shoulder, cut into 5-inch chunks

1 head of garlic, halved at the equator

1 onion, quartered

2 bay leaves

5 sprigs of fresh thyme

4 oz. salt

10 cups water

5 cups Spicy BBQ Sauce (see page 252)

Pickled Red Onions (see page 251), for serving

Honey Cornbread (see page 37), for serving

1   Preheat the oven to 365°F. Place all of the ingredients, except for the pickled onions and cornbread, in a large roasting pan and bring it to a simmer over medium heat. Cook for 10 minutes.

2   Cover the roasting pan with aluminum foil, place it in the oven, and cook until the pork is very tender, about 2 hours.

3   Remove the pork from the oven and use two forks to shred it. Serve with the pickled onions and cornbread and enjoy.

BUTTER CHICKEN

INGREDIENTS

¼ cup coconut oil

1 lb. chicken legs

1 lb. bone-in, skin-on chicken thighs

Salt and pepper, to taste

1 yellow onion, minced

2 garlic cloves, minced

1 tablespoon turmeric

2 teaspoons cayenne pepper

1 tablespoon paprika

½ tablespoon cumin

½ tablespoon coriander

½ teaspoon ground ginger

¼ teaspoon cinnamon

2 cups coconut milk

5 cups Chicken Stock (see page 237)

Fresh cilantro, chopped, for garnish

White rice, cooked, for serving

1   Place the coconut oil in a large, deep skillet and warm it over medium-high heat. Season the chicken with salt and pepper and add it to the pan in batches, taking care not to crowd the pan. Cook the chicken until it is browned all over, turning it as necessary. Remove the chicken from the pan and set it aside.

2   Reduce the heat to low, add the onion and garlic, and cook, stirring occasionally, until the onion has softened, about 6 minutes.

3   Stir in the turmeric, cayenne, paprika, cumin, coriander, ginger, and cinnamon and cook, stirring continually, for 2 minutes.

4   Return the chicken to the pan, add the coconut milk and stock, and bring to a simmer. Cook until the chicken is cooked through and very tender, about 35 minutes.

5   Remove the chicken from the pan, remove the meat from the bones, and chop it. Stir the chicken back into the pan, garnish the dish with cilantro, and serve with rice.

FRIED CHICKEN

INGREDIENTS

4 lb. chicken, broken down

¼ yellow onion, sliced

2 garlic cloves, smashed

1 cup buttermilk

1 teaspoon kosher salt

½ teaspoon garlic powder

½ teaspoon onion powder

½ teaspoon black pepper

¼ teaspoon cayenne powder

3 cups all-purpose flour

1 cup cornstarch

Canola oil, as needed

1 Place the chicken in a large baking pan, add the onion, garlic, and buttermilk, and let the chicken marinate for 30 minutes.

2 Place all of the remaining ingredients, except for the canola oil, in a baking dish and stir until well combined.

3 Add canola oil to a Dutch oven until it is about 2 inches deep and warm it to 350°F. Place a wire rack in a baking sheet.

4 Dredge the chicken in the seasoned flour until it is completely coated. Let the chicken rest on the wire rack.

5 Gently slip the chicken into the hot oil and fry until it is golden brown and 160°F in the center, about 15 minutes, turning it every 5 minutes. Remove the chicken from the hot oil to the wire rack and let it drain and rest for 10 minutes before serving.

EMPANADAS

INGREDIENTS

For the Dough

¼ teaspoon kosher salt

6 tablespoons warm water (110°F)

1½ cups all-purpose flour, plus more as needed

3 tablespoons lard or unsalted butter, cut into small pieces

For the Filling

2 teaspoons extra-virgin olive oil

1 yellow onion, minced

1 garlic clove, minced

¾ lb. ground pork

1 (14 oz.) can of crushed tomatoes

½ teaspoon kosher salt

¼ teaspoon black pepper

1 cinnamon stick

2 whole cloves

2 tablespoons raisins

2 teaspoons apple cider vinegar

2 tablespoons slivered almonds, toasted

Canola oil, as needed

1 To prepare the dough, dissolve the salt in the warm water. Place the flour in a mixing bowl, add the lard or butter, and work the mixture with a pastry blender until it is coarse crumbs. Add the salted water and knead the mixture until it comes together as a stiff dough. Cut the dough into eight pieces, cover them with plastic wrap, and chill in the refrigerator for 20 minutes.

2 To prepare the filling, place the olive oil in a skillet and warm it over medium heat. Add the onion and cook, stirring occasionally, until it has softened, about 5 minutes. Add the garlic and cook, stirring continually, for 1 minute, and then add the ground pork. Cook, breaking it up, until it is light brown, about 5 minutes. Drain off any excess fat and add the tomatoes, salt, pepper, cinnamon stick, cloves, raisins, and vinegar. Simmer until the filling is thick, about 30 minutes. Remove from heat and let cool before folding in the toasted almonds.

3 Add canola oil to a Dutch oven until it is 2 inches deep and warm it to 350°F. Preheat the oven to 160°F and place a platter in the oven.

4 Place the pieces of dough on a flour-dusted work surface and roll each one into a 5-inch circle. Place 3 tablespoons of the filling in the center of one circle, brush the edge with water, and fold into a half-moon. Crimp the edge to seal the empanada tight, pressing down on the filling to remove as much air as possible. Repeat with the remaining filling and pieces of dough.

5 Gently slip half of the empanadas into the hot oil and fry until golden brown, about 5 minutes. Drain the fried empanadas on a paper towel-lined plate and place them in the warm oven while you cook the remaining empanadas.

NEW YORK–STYLE PIZZA

INGREDIENTS

⅛ teaspoon instant yeast

6¾ oz. water

10.9 oz. bread flour or "00" flour, plus more as needed

1½ teaspoons fine sea salt

Extra-virgin olive oil, as needed

Semolina flour, as needed

1 cup Marinara Sauce (see page 243)

3 cups shredded mozzarella cheese

Dried oregano, to taste

1   In a large bowl, combine the yeast, bread or "00" flour, and water. Work the mixture until it just holds together. Dust a work surface with bread or "00" flour and knead the dough until it is compact, smooth, and elastic.

2   Add the salt and knead the dough until it is developed and elastic, meaning it pulls back when stretched. Transfer the dough to an airtight container and let it rest at room temperature for 2 hours.

3   Divide the dough into two pieces and shape them into very tight balls. Place the balls of dough in a baking dish with high edges, leaving enough space between the rounds that they won't touch when fully risen. Coat a piece of plastic wrap with olive oil, place it over the rounds, and let them rest until they have doubled in size, about 6 hours.

4   Place a baking stone on the middle rack of the oven and preheat the oven to the maximum temperature. Dust a work surface with semolina flour, place the balls of dough on the surface, and gently stretch them into 10- to 12-inch rounds. Cover them with the sauce and top with the mozzarella. Season with oregano and drizzle olive oil over the pizzas.

5   Using a peel or a flat baking sheet, transfer one pizza at a time to the heated baking stone in the oven. Bake for about 15 minutes, until the crust is golden brown and starting to char. Remove, repeat with the other pizza, and let both cool slightly before serving.

KALBI

INGREDIENTS

1½ cups cola

¾ cup sugar

2 tablespoons rice vinegar

½ cup low-sodium soy sauce

1 tablespoon onion powder

1 Asian pear, sliced thin

2 garlic cloves, minced

½-inch piece of fresh ginger, peeled and grated

2 tablespoons sesame oil

7 tablespoons brown sugar

5 flanken-style short ribs

Scallions, chopped, for garnish

Kimchi (see page 253), for serving

1 Place the cola, sugar, rice vinegar, soy sauce, onion powder, pear, garlic, ginger, sesame oil, and brown sugar in a blender and puree until smooth.

2 Place the short ribs in a baking dish and pour the marinade over them. Let the short ribs marinate for 30 minutes.

3 Prepare a gas or charcoal grill for medium-high heat (about 450°F). Place the short ribs on the grill and cook until they are caramelized and cooked through, making sure to turn them frequently to keep them from burning.

4 Remove the short ribs from the grill and let them rest for 10 minutes. Garnish with scallions, serve with Kimchi, and enjoy.

PIERNA DE PUERCO

INGREDIENTS

2 ancho chile peppers, stems and seeds removed

1 dried cascabel chile pepper, stem and seeds removed

1 chipotle morita chile pepper, stem and seeds removed

1 guajillo chile pepper, stem and seeds removed

½ teaspoon black peppercorns

1½ teaspoons coriander seeds

1 teaspoon cumin seeds

½ teaspoon cinnamon

½ teaspoon ground cloves

8 garlic cloves, chopped

½ cup white vinegar

1 cup mezcal

Salt, to taste

3 lbs. pork shoulder, cut into 1-inch cubes

½ white onion, chopped

4 bay leaves

1 tablespoon all-purpose flour

White rice, cooked, for serving

1. Place the chiles in a bowl of hot water and let them soak for 20 minutes.

2. Place the peppercorns, coriander, and cumin in a dry skillet and toast until fragrant, shaking the pan frequently to prevent the aromatics from burning.

3. Drain the chiles and place them in a blender along with the toasted aromatics, cinnamon, cloves, garlic, vinegar, and mezcal. Puree until smooth and season the puree generously with salt.

4. Place the pork shoulder in a large baking dish, rub the puree over it, and let it marinate in the refrigerator for 1 hour.

5. Place the pork shoulder and marinade in a large saucepan, add water until the pork shoulder is covered, and add the onion and bay leaves to the pan. Bring the water to a boil, reduce the heat so that the water simmers, and cook the pork until it is fork-tender, about 1 hour.

6. Stir in the flour and cook until the sauce has thickened slightly. Taste, adjust the seasoning as needed, and serve with rice.

BEEF & PORK CHEESEBURGERS

INGREDIENTS

1 lb. ground beef

1 lb. ground pork

Salt and pepper, to taste

2 tablespoons unsalted butter

2 sweet onions, sliced thin

½ cup mayonnaise

6 brioche buns, toasted

6 slices of cheddar cheese

1   Place the beef and pork in a mixing bowl and season the mixture with salt and pepper. Stir to combine, cover the bowl with plastic wrap, and place it in the refrigerator.

2   Place the butter in a skillet and melt it over medium-low heat.

3   Add the onions and a pinch of salt and cook, stirring occasionally, until the onions develop a deep brown color, 20 to 30 minutes. Remove the pan from heat and let the onions cool completely.

4   Transfer the cooled onions to a food processor and blitz until smooth. Place the puree and mayonnaise in a mixing bowl, season the mixture with salt and pepper, and stir to combine. Chill the mixture in the refrigerator for 2 hours.

5   When ready to serve, prepare a gas or charcoal grill for medium-high heat (about 450°F) or place a cast-iron skillet over medium-high heat. Divide the beef-and-pork mixture into 6 balls and then gently shape them into patties.

6   Place the burgers on the grill or in the skillet and cook for 8 to 10 minutes. Flip the burgers over and cook until cooked through, 5 to 8 minutes. Since you are working with pork, it is important to cook the burgers all the way through. If you're worried that they will dry out, don't fret. The pork fat will keep the burgers moist and flavorful.

7   Spread the mayonnaise on one half of a bun. Place the burgers on another half of the toasted buns, top them with the slices of cheese, assemble the burgers, and enjoy.

MAC & CHEESE WITH BROWN BUTTER BREAD CRUMBS

INGREDIENTS

Salt, to taste

1 lb. elbow macaroni

7 tablespoons unsalted butter

2 cups panko

½ yellow onion, minced

3 tablespoons all-purpose flour

1 tablespoon yellow mustard

1 teaspoon turmeric

1 teaspoon garlic powder

1 teaspoon white pepper

2 cups light cream

2 cups whole milk

1 lb. American cheese, sliced

10 oz. Boursin cheese

½ lb. extra-sharp cheddar cheese, sliced

1   Preheat the oven to 400°F. Fill a Dutch oven with water and bring it to a boil. Add salt and the macaroni and cook until the macaroni is just shy of al dente, about 6 minutes. Drain and set aside.

2   Place the pot over medium heat and add 3 tablespoons of the butter. Cook until the butter starts to give off a nutty smell and browns. Add the panko, stir, and cook until it starts to look like wet sand, about 4 minutes. Remove the panko from the pot and set it aside.

3   Wipe out the Dutch oven, place it over medium-high heat, and add the onion and the remaining butter. Cook, stirring occasionally, until the onion is soft, about 10 minutes. Gradually add the flour, stirring constantly to prevent lumps from forming. Stir in the mustard, turmeric, garlic powder, white pepper, cream, and milk, reduce the heat to medium, and bring to a simmer.

4   Add the cheeses one at a time, stirring to incorporate before adding the next one. When all of the cheeses have been incorporated and the mixture is smooth, cook the mixture until the flour taste is completely gone, about 10 minutes. Stir in the macaroni and top the mixture with the panko.

5   Place the Dutch oven in the oven and bake until the panko is crispy and golden brown, 10 to 15 minutes.

6   Remove the pot from the oven and serve immediately.

MOUSSAKA

1   Preheat the oven to 350°F. To begin preparations for the filling, place 4 cups of cold water in a bowl, add the salt, and stir. When the salt has dissolved, add the eggplant cubes and let the cubes soak for about 20 minutes. Drain the eggplant and rinse with cold water. Squeeze the cubes to remove as much water as you can, place them on a pile of paper towels, and blot them dry. Set aside.

2   While the eggplants are soaking, add 1 tablespoon of the olive oil to a large cast-iron skillet and warm it over medium-high heat. Add the ground lamb and cook, using a wooden spoon to break it up, until it is browned, about 8 minutes. Transfer the cooked lamb to a bowl and set it aside.

3   Add 2 tablespoons of the olive oil and the eggplant cubes to the skillet and cook, stirring frequently until they start to brown, about 5 minutes. Transfer the cooked eggplant to the bowl containing the lamb and add the remaining olive oil, the onions, and garlic to the skillet. Cook, stirring frequently, until the onions are translucent, about 3 minutes. Return the lamb and eggplants to the skillet and stir in the wine,

sauce, parsley, oregano, and cinnamon. Reduce the heat to low and simmer for about 15 minutes, stirring occasionally. Season with salt, pepper, and nutmeg and transfer the mixture to a 13 x 9-inch baking dish.

4   To begin preparations for the crust, place the eggs in a large bowl and beat them lightly. Place a saucepan over medium heat and melt the butter. Reduce the heat to medium-low and add the flour. Stir constantly until the mixture is smooth.

5   While stirring constantly, gradually add the milk and bring the mixture to a boil. When the mixture reaches a boil, remove the pan from heat. Stir approximately half of the mixture in the saucepan into the beaten eggs. Stir the tempered eggs into the saucepan and then add the cheese and dill or parsley. Stir to combine and pour the mixture over the lamb mixture in the baking dish, using a rubber spatula to smooth the top.

6   Place the baking dish in the oven and bake the moussaka until the crust is set and golden brown, about 35 minutes. Remove from the oven and let the moussaka rest for 5 minutes before serving.

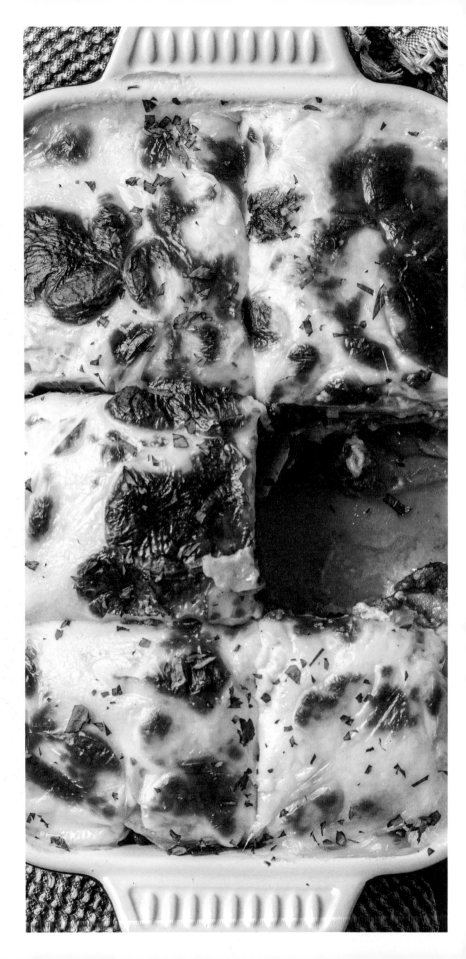

INGREDIENTS

For the Filling

¼ cup kosher salt, plus more
to taste

3 large eggplants, trimmed,
cut into cubes

5 tablespoons extra-virgin
olive oil

2 lbs. ground lamb

2 onions, diced

3 garlic cloves, minced

½ cup dry white wine

1 cup Marinara Sauce
(see page 243)

2 tablespoons chopped fresh
parsley

1 teaspoon dried oregano

½ teaspoon cinnamon

Black pepper, to taste

Freshly grated nutmeg, to taste

For the Crust

5 eggs

6 tablespoons unsalted butter

⅓ cup all-purpose flour

2½ cups milk

⅔ cup grated kefalotyri cheese

⅓ cup fresh dill or parsley,
chopped

BOLOGNESE WITH PENNE

INGREDIENTS

2 tablespoons extra-virgin olive oil

½ lb. bacon, chopped

1½ lbs. ground beef

Salt and pepper, to taste

1 onion, chopped

1 carrot, peeled and minced

3 celery stalks, chopped

2 garlic cloves, minced

1 tablespoon fresh thyme

1 cup sherry

8 cups crushed tomatoes

1 cup heavy cream

2 tablespoons finely chopped
fresh sage

1 lb. penne

4 tablespoons unsalted butter

1 cup freshly grated Parmesan
cheese, plus more for garnish

Fresh basil, for garnish

Red pepper flakes, for garnish
(optional)

1   Place the olive oil and bacon in a Dutch oven and cook the bacon over medium heat until it is crispy, 6 to 8 minutes. Add the beef, season the mixture with salt and pepper, and cook, breaking the beef up with a wooden spoon as it browns, until it is cooked through, about 8 minutes.

2   Remove the bacon and beef from the pot and set the mixture aside.

3   Add the onion, carrot, celery, and garlic to the Dutch oven, season the mixture with salt, and cook, stirring frequently, until the carrot is tender, about 8 minutes. Return the bacon and beef to the pot, stir in the thyme and sherry, and cook until the sherry has nearly evaporated.

4   Add the crushed tomatoes, reduce the heat to low, and cook the sauce for about 45 minutes, stirring often, until it has thickened to the desired consistency.

5   Stir the cream and sage into the sauce and gently simmer for another 15 minutes.

6   Bring water to a boil in a large saucepan. Add salt and the penne and cook until it is just shy of al dente, about 6 minutes. Reserve ½ cup of the pasta water, drain the penne, and then return it to the pan. Add the butter, sauce, and reserved pasta water and stir to combine. Add the Parmesan and stir it has until melted.

7   Garnish the dish with additional Parmesan, basil, and red pepper flakes (if desired) and enjoy.

CAPRESE CHICKEN

INGREDIENTS

1 garlic clove, minced

1 teaspoon dried oregano

1 teaspoon garlic powder

Salt and pepper, to taste

2 tablespoons extra-virgin olive oil

2 lbs. boneless, skinless chicken breasts, halved at their equators

1 lb. tomatoes, sliced

1 lb. fresh mozzarella cheese, drained and sliced

Leaves from 1 bunch of fresh basil

Balsamic vinegar, for garnish

1 Preheat the oven to 375°F. Place the garlic, oregano, garlic powder, salt, and pepper in a bowl and stir to combine. Place 1 tablespoon of the olive oil and the sliced chicken breasts in a bowl and toss to coat. Set them aside.

2 Coat the bottom of a large cast-iron skillet with the remaining olive oil and warm it over medium-high heat. Working in batches, sear the chicken breasts for 1 minute on each side.

3 When all of the chicken has been seared, place half of the breasts in an even layer on the bottom of the skillet. Top with two-thirds of the tomatoes and mozzarella, and half of the basil leaves. Place the remaining chicken breasts on top in an even layer and cover this layer of chicken with the remaining tomatoes, mozzarella, and basil.

4 Place the skillet in the oven and cook until the interior temperature of the chicken breasts is 165°F, about 10 minutes.

5 Remove the skillet from the oven and let the chicken rest for 10 minutes. Drizzle the balsamic vinegar over the dish and enjoy.

SHRIMP & GRITS

INGREDIENTS

4 cups water

1 cup quick-cooking grits

2 large eggs

5 tablespoons unsalted butter, softened

¾ cup milk

Salt and pepper, to taste

1 lb. cheddar cheese, grated

1 tablespoon extra-virgin olive oil

1 lb. shrimp, shells removed, deveined

2 garlic cloves, minced

1 tablespoon fresh lemon juice

2 dashes of Tabasco

1 Preheat the oven to 425°F. Place the water in a large cast-iron skillet and bring it to a boil. While stirring constantly, slowly pour in the grits. Cover the pan, reduce the heat to low, and cook, while stirring occasionally, until the grits are quite thick, about 5 minutes. Remove the pan from heat.

2 Place the eggs, 4 tablespoons of the butter, and the milk in a bowl, season the mixture with salt and pepper, and stir to combine. Stir the cooked grits into the egg mixture, add three-quarters of the cheese, and stir to incorporate.

3 Wipe out the skillet, coat it with the remaining butter, and pour the grits mixture into the skillet. Place the skillet in the oven and bake for 30 minutes. Remove, sprinkle the remaining cheese on top, and return the grits to the oven. Bake until the cheese is melted and the grits are firm, about 15 minutes. Remove the grits from the oven and let them cool for 10 minutes.

4 Place the olive oil in a medium cast-iron skillet and warm it over medium-high heat. Add the shrimp to the skillet, season them with salt and pepper, and cook for 1 minute. Turn the shrimp over, stir in the garlic, lemon juice, and Tabasco, and cook until the shrimp are pink and opaque throughout, 1 to 2 minutes.

5 Divide the grits among four bowls, place a few shrimp on top of each portion, and enjoy.

SKILLET LASAGNA

INGREDIENTS

2 tablespoons extra-virgin olive oil

1 onion, sliced thin

4 garlic cloves, sliced thin

2 zucchini, chopped

1 cup chopped eggplant

2 cups baby spinach

1 (28 oz.) can of whole peeled San Marzano tomatoes, with their liquid, crushed by hand

Salt and pepper, to taste

8 no-cook lasagna noodles

1 cup ricotta cheese

½ cup freshly grated Parmesan cheese, plus more for garnish

½ lb. fresh mozzarella cheese, shredded

Fresh basil, finely chopped, for garnish

1 Place the olive oil in a large cast-iron skillet and warm it over medium-low heat. Add the onion and cook, stirring occasionally, until it has softened, about 6 minutes.

2 Add the garlic and cook, stirring continually, for 1 minute. Raise the heat to medium, add the zucchini and eggplant, and cook, stirring occasionally, until the zucchini has softened and the eggplant has collapsed, about 10 minutes.

3 Add the spinach and cook, stirring continually, until it has wilted, about 2 minutes. Transfer the vegetable mixture to a bowl.

4 Cover the bottom of the skillet with a thin layer of the tomatoes and season them with salt and pepper. Top with 4 lasagna noodles, breaking off the edges as necessary to fit the pan. Spread half of the vegetable mixture over the noodles and dot the mixture with dollops of ricotta. Top with one-third of the remaining tomatoes, season them with salt and pepper, and spread the remaining vegetable mixture over the top. Dot the vegetables with dollops of the remaining ricotta. Top with the remaining lasagna noodles, spread the remaining tomatoes over the top, and then layer the Parmesan and mozzarella over the tomatoes.

5 Season with salt and pepper, cover the skillet, and cook over medium-low heat until the pasta is soft and the cheese has completely melted, 5 to 10 minutes.

6 Uncover the skillet, raise the heat to medium-high, and cook until the sauce has thickened, about 5 minutes. Remove the pan from heat and let the lasagna cool slightly, 5 to 10 minutes, before cutting. Sprinkle the basil over the lasagna and enjoy.

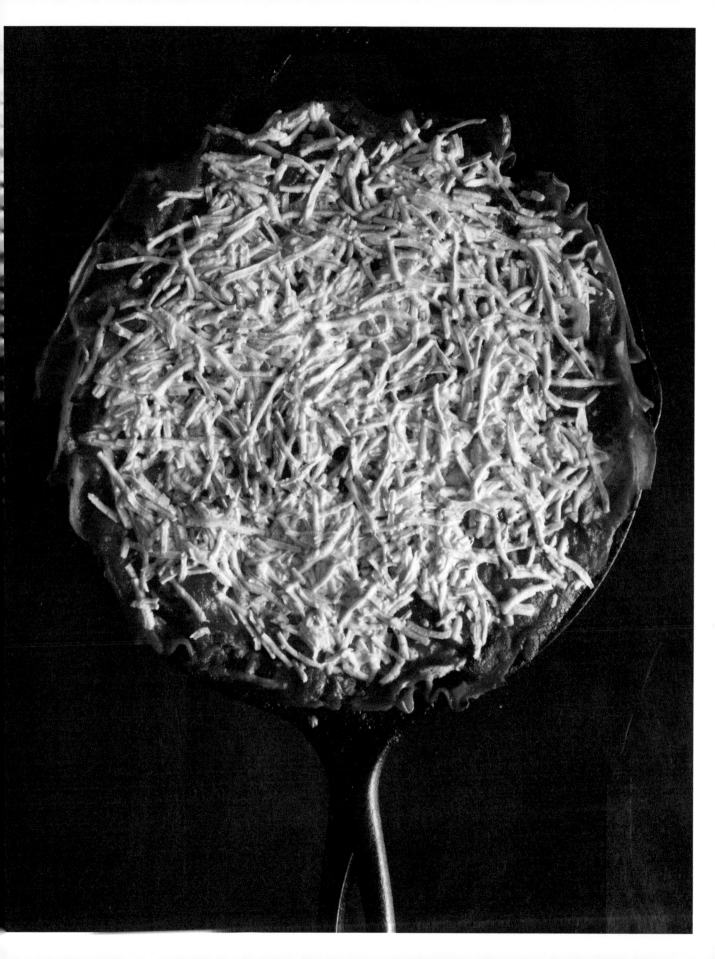

FETTUCCINE ALFREDO

INGREDIENTS

Salt and pepper, to taste

¾ lb. fettuccine

½ cup heavy cream

2½ tablespoons unsalted butter, at room temperature

1 cup grated Parmesan cheese, plus more for garnish

½ teaspoon freshly grated nutmeg

1   Bring a large pot of water to a boil. Once it's boiling, add salt and the fettuccine and cook for 6 minutes. Reserve ½ cup of pasta water and drain the fettuccine. Set it aside.

2   Place the reserved pasta water and heavy cream in a large skillet and bring it to a simmer. Add the butter and stir until it has been emulsified. Gradually incorporate the Parmesan, making sure each addition has melted before adding the next.

3   Add the fettuccine to the skillet and toss to combine. Sprinkle the nutmeg over the top, garnish the dish with additional Parmesan, and season it with pepper before serving.

SHAKSHUKA

INGREDIENTS

2 tablespoons extra-virgin olive oil

1 onion, chopped

2 green bell peppers, stems and seeds removed, chopped

2 garlic cloves, minced

1 teaspoon coriander

1 teaspoon sweet paprika

½ teaspoon cumin

1 teaspoon turmeric

Pinch of red pepper flakes

2 tablespoons tomato paste

5 ripe tomatoes, chopped

Salt and pepper, to taste

6 eggs

1 cup crumbled feta cheese

¼ cup chopped fresh parsley, for garnish

¼ cup chopped fresh mint, for garnish

1   Place the olive oil in a large cast-iron skillet and warm it over medium heat. Add the onion and cook, stirring occasionally, until it has softened, about 5 minutes. Add the bell peppers and cook, stirring occasionally, until they have softened, about 5 minutes.

2   Add the garlic, coriander, paprika, cumin, turmeric, red pepper flakes, and tomato paste and cook, stirring continually, for 1 minute. Add the tomatoes and bring the mixture to a boil. Reduce the heat, cover the pan, and simmer for 15 minutes.

3   Remove the cover and cook until the shakshuka has reduced slightly, about 5 minutes.

4   Season the shakshuka with salt and pepper. Using the back of a wooden spoon, make six wells in the mixture. Crack an egg into each well and sprinkle the feta over the shakshuka.

5   Reduce the heat to a simmer, cover the pan, and cook until the egg whites are set, 6 to 8 minutes.

6   Remove the pan from heat, garnish with the parsley and mint, and enjoy.

CHICKEN PANINI WITH SUN-DRIED TOMATO AIOLI

INGREDIENTS

For the Aioli

1 cup sun-dried tomatoes in olive oil, drained and chopped

1 cup mayonnaise

1 tablespoon whole-grain mustard

2 tablespoons finely chopped fresh parsley

2 tablespoons minced scallions

1 teaspoon white balsamic vinegar

1 garlic clove, minced

2 teaspoons kosher salt

1 teaspoon black pepper

For the Sandwiches

8 slices of crusty bread

8 slices of cheddar cheese

2 leftover cooked chicken breasts, sliced

12 slices of cooked bacon

1 cup arugula

1   Preheat a panini press. To prepare the aioli, place all of the ingredients in a mixing bowl and stir until combined.

2   To begin preparations for the sandwiches, spread some of the aioli on each slice of bread. Place a slice of cheddar on each slice of bread. Divide the chicken between four pieces of the bread. Top each portion of chicken with 3 slices of bacon and ¼ cup of the arugula and assemble the sandwiches.

3   Place the sandwiches in the panini press and press until the cheese has melted and there is a nice crust on the bread. Remove the sandwiches from the panini press and enjoy immediately.

TIP: If you don't have a panini press, don't worry. Simply place 1 tablespoon of olive oil in a large skillet and warm over medium-high heat. Place a sandwich in the pan, place a warmed cast-iron skillet on top so it is pressing down on the sandwich, and cook until golden brown. Turn the sandwich over and repeat.

TINGA DE POLLO

INGREDIENTS

2 bone-in, skin-on chicken legs

2 bone-in, skin-on chicken thighs

2 tablespoons kosher salt, plus more to taste

2 bay leaves

1 tablespoon extra-virgin olive oil

1 white onion, sliced thin

1 garlic clove, sliced thin

3 large tomatoes, diced

2 chipotle chile peppers, stems and seeds removed

Corn Tortillas (see page 240), warmed, for serving

Pickled Red Onions (see page 251), for serving

Queso fresco, for serving

1 Place the chicken in a large pot and cover with cold water by at least an inch. Add the salt and bay leaves and bring the water to a simmer. Cook the chicken until the meat pulls away from the bone, about 40 minutes.

2 While the chicken is simmering, place the olive oil in a large skillet and warm over medium heat. Add the onion and garlic and cook, stirring frequently, until the onion is translucent, about 3 minutes. Reduce the heat to low and cook until the onion has softened.

3 Add the diced tomatoes and cook, stirring occasionally, for another 5 minutes.

4 Shred the chicken and reserve 2 cups of the cooking liquid. Place the chiles in a bowl with 1 cup of the cooking liquid and let them sit until they have softened, about 20 minutes.

5 Chop the chiles, add them to the skillet along with the shredded chicken, and cook, stirring occasionally, until the flavor has developed to your liking, about 8 minutes. Add the remaining cooking liquid to the pan if it becomes too dry.

6 Season with salt and serve with tortillas, pickled onions, and queso fresco.

CHAR SIU

INGREDIENTS

¼ cup Hoisin Sauce
(see page 254)

1 tablespoon dark soy sauce

2 tablespoons Shaoxing wine

2 tablespoons ketchup

1 tablespoon oyster sauce

¼ cup sugar

2 teaspoons kosher salt

3 pinches of curing salt

1 teaspoon five-spice powder

1 teaspoon red food coloring
(optional)

4 lbs. boneless pork shoulder,
cut with the grain into 3 or 4
long strips

¼ cup honey

1 Place all of the ingredients, except for the pork and honey, in a large bowl and stir until well combined. Add the pork and massage the marinade into the meat. Cover the bowl and marinate the pork in the refrigerator for 48 hours.

2 Preheat the oven to 375°F, placing a pan filled with water on the floor of the oven.

3 Place the pork on a baking sheet and reserve the marinade. Place the pork in the oven and roast for 25 to 30 minutes.

4 Place the reserved marinade in a bowl, stir in the honey, and set the mixture aside.

5 Turn the pork over, brush it with the marinade, and roast for another 20 minutes. Turn the pork over, brush with more of the marinade, and roast until the pork is cooked through, 15 to 20 minutes.

6 Remove the pork from the oven and let it rest for 20 minutes before slicing and serving.

MUFFULETTA

INGREDIENTS

1 red bell pepper

1 cup sun-dried tomatoes in olive oil, drained and chopped

1 cup pitted green olives, chopped

1 cup pitted black olives, chopped

¼ cup extra-virgin olive oil

¼ cup chopped fresh parsley

2 tablespoons fresh lemon juice

1 teaspoon dried oregano

1 loaf of Italian or French bread, halved lengthwise

2 cups torn lettuce

4 oz. mortadella, sliced thin

4 oz. provolone cheese, sliced thin

4 oz. soppressata, sliced thin

1 Preheat the oven to 400°F. Place the bell pepper on a baking sheet, place it in the oven, and roast, turning it occasionally, until it is charred all over, about 25 minutes. Remove the pepper from the oven and let it cool. When cool enough to handle, remove the charred skin, chop the pepper, and discard the seeds and stem. Place the roasted pepper in a mixing bowl.

2 Add the tomatoes, olives, olive oil, parsley, lemon juice, and oregano to the bowl. Cover and refrigerate overnight.

3 Drain the olive mixture and reserve the liquid. Remove most of the crumb from one of the halves of the bread and generously brush the cut sides with the reserved liquid. Fill the piece of bread with the crumb removed with half of the olive mixture and top with half of the lettuce and all the mortadella, provolone, and soppressata.

4 Layer the remaining lettuce over the soppressata and top with the remaining olive mixture and the other piece of bread. Wrap the sandwich in plastic wrap and place it on a large plate. Place another plate on top and weigh it down with a good-sized cookbook or something similar. Refrigerate for at least 1 hour before slicing and serving.

OYSTER SLIDERS WITH RED PEPPER MAYO

INGREDIENTS

3 red bell peppers

Canola oil, as needed

1 cup cornmeal

Salt, to taste

½ lb. shucked oysters

2 eggs, beaten

1 tablespoon unsalted butter

4 King's Hawaiian Rolls, split open

½ cup mayonnaise

1 Preheat the oven to 400°F. Place the red peppers on a baking sheet, place them in the oven, and roast, turning them occasionally, until the peppers are blistered all over, 35 to 40 minutes. Remove them from the oven and let them cool. When cool enough to handle, remove the skins, stems, and seeds from the peppers and set the roasted flesh aside.

2 Add canola oil to a Dutch oven until it is about 1 inch deep and warm it to 350°F.

3 Place the cornmeal and salt in a bowl and stir to combine. Dredge the oysters in the beaten eggs and then in the cornmeal-and-salt mixture. Repeat until the oysters are completely coated.

4 Gently slip the oysters into the hot oil and fry until they are crispy and golden brown, 3 to 5 minutes. Transfer the fried oysters to a paper towel-lined plate to drain.

5 Place the butter in a skillet and melt over medium heat. Place the buns in the skillet, cut side down, and toast until lightly browned. Remove the buns from the pan and set them aside.

6 Place the roasted peppers and mayonnaise in a blender and puree until smooth. Spread the mayonnaise on the buns, sandwich the fried oysters between the buns, and enjoy.

STUFFED PEPPERS

INGREDIENTS

4 bell peppers, stems and seeds removed

1½ cups Chicken Stock (see page 237)

¾ cup rice, rinsed and drained

½ lb. ground Italian sausage

2 onions, diced

6 garlic cloves, minced

½ teaspoon dried oregano

Salt and pepper, to taste

⅛ teaspoon red pepper flakes

1 (28 oz.) can of crushed tomatoes

2 tablespoons chopped fresh basil

1¼ cups freshly grated Parmesan cheese

1 Preheat the oven to 350°F. Cut the top ¼ inch of the peppers off, set the tops aside, remove the seeds, and place the peppers in a square baking dish.

2 Place the stock and rice in a medium saucepan and bring to a simmer over medium heat. Reduce the heat to low, cover the pan, and cook until the rice is almost tender and has absorbed the stock, 13 to 15 minutes.

3 Place the sausage in a large skillet and cook over medium-high heat until it is browned all over, about 8 minutes, breaking it up with a fork as it cooks. Using a slotted spoon, transfer the sausage to a bowl.

4 Place the onions in the skillet and cook, stirring occasionally, until they start to brown, 8 to 10 minutes. Stir in the garlic, oregano, salt, pepper, and red pepper flakes and cook until fragrant, about 30 seconds. Add the tomatoes, bring the mixture to a boil, and remove the pan from heat. Stir the basil into the sauce, taste, and adjust the seasoning as necessary.

5 Place 1 cup of the sauce and 1 cup of the Parmesan in the bowl with the sausage and stir until thoroughly combined. Fill the peppers with the mixture, sprinkle some of the remaining Parmesan over each one, and place the tops back on the peppers.

6 Place the stuffed peppers in the oven and bake until the peppers are tender, about 25 minutes. Warm the remaining sauce while the peppers are in the oven, and set the tops back on each one.

7 Remove the peppers from the oven, spoon some of the remaining sauce over each one, and enjoy.

SKILLET MEATLOAF WITH BACON

INGREDIENTS

1½ lbs. ground beef

½ lb. ground pork

1 yellow onion, minced

2 teaspoons garlic powder

1 cup bread crumbs

¼ cup whole milk

2 eggs, lightly beaten

2 tablespoons tomato paste

2 tablespoons Worcestershire sauce

2 teaspoons extra-virgin olive oil

8 slices of thick-cut bacon

1. Preheat the oven to 375°F. Place the beef, pork, onion, garlic powder, bread crumbs, milk, eggs, tomato paste, and Worcestershire sauce in a bowl and work the mixture with your hands until it is thoroughly combined.

2. Coat a 10-inch cast-iron skillet with the olive oil. Place the meat mixture in the pan and form it into a dome. Lay four slices of the bacon lengthwise over the top and place the remaining four on top crosswise, weaving them together.

3. Place the skillet in the oven and bake until the interior of the meatloaf is about 150°F, about 45 minutes.

4. Remove the meatloaf from the oven and let cool for 10 minutes before slicing.

PORK FRIED RICE

INGREDIENTS

¼ cup canola oil

1-inch piece of fresh ginger, peeled and minced

2 garlic cloves, minced

3 large eggs

2 cups minced carrots

4 cups leftover white rice

4 scallions, trimmed and chopped

1 cup peas

2 tablespoons soy sauce

1 tablespoon rice vinegar

1 tablespoon fish sauce

1 tablespoon sesame oil

2 cups chopped leftover roast pork

1   Place the canola oil in a 12-inch cast-iron skillet and warm over medium-high heat. When the oil starts to shimmer, add the ginger and garlic and cook until they just start to brown, about 2 minutes.

2   Add the eggs and scramble until the eggs are set, about 2 minutes. Add the carrots, rice, scallions, and peas and stir to incorporate.

3   Add the soy sauce, rice vinegar, fish sauce, sesame oil, and pork and cook, while stirring constantly, for 5 minutes. Serve immediately.

DESSERTS

Desserts, due to the traditions, memories, and emotions attached to them, provide a tremendous amount of comfort. Things being what they are, it is always better to take matters into your own hands when your palate sounds a cry for something sweet. Not only is a homemade dessert more likely to satiate, since you can tailor it exactly to your tastes, but taking a step back from the busy world to turn out something special means your satisfaction won't be limited to your consumption of it.

YIELD: 1 CAKE • **ACTIVE TIME:** 1 HOUR • **TOTAL TIME:** 3 HOURS AND 30 MINUTES

CHOCOLATE CAKE

1 Preheat the oven to 350°F. Line three round 8-inch cake pans with parchment paper and coat them with nonstick cooking spray.

2 To begin preparations for the cake, sift the sugar, flour, cocoa powder, baking soda, baking powder, and salt into a medium bowl. Set the mixture aside.

3 In the work bowl of a stand mixer fitted with the whisk attachment, combine the sour cream, canola oil, and eggs on medium speed.

4 Reduce the speed to low, add the dry mixture, and whisk until combined. Scrape the side of the bowl with a rubber spatula as needed. Add the hot coffee and whisk until thoroughly incorporated.

5 Pour 1½ cups of batter into each cake pan. Bang the pans on the countertop to spread the batter and to remove any possible air bubbles.

6 Place the cakes in the oven and bake until lightly golden brown and baked through, 25 to 30 minutes. Insert a cake tester in the center of each cake to check for doneness.

7 Remove from the oven and place the cakes on a wire rack. Let them cool completely.

8 To prepare the filling, place 2 cups of the butterfluff and the cocoa powder in a small bowl and whisk to combine.

9 To prepare the frosting, place the buttercream and cocoa powder in another mixing bowl and whisk until combined. Set the mixtures aside.

10 Trim a thin layer off the tops of each cake to create a flat surface. Transfer 2 cups of the frosting to a piping bag and cut a ½-inch slit in it.

11 Place one cake on a cake stand and pipe one ring of frosting around the edge. Place 1 cup of the filling in the center and level it with an offset spatula. Place the second cake on top and repeat the process with the frosting and filling. Place the last cake on top, place 1½ cups of the frosting on the cake and frost the top and side of the cake using an offset spatula. Refrigerate the cake for at least 1 hour.

12 Carefully spoon some of the ganache over the edge of the cake so that it drips down. Spread any remaining ganache over the center of the cake.

13 Place the cake in the refrigerator for 30 minutes so that the ganache hardens. To serve, sprinkle the curls of chocolate over the top and slice.

INGREDIENTS

For the Cakes

20 oz. sugar

13 oz. all-purpose flour

4 oz. cocoa powder

1 tablespoon baking soda

1½ teaspoon baking powder

1½ teaspoon kosher salt

1½ cups sour cream

¾ cup canola oil

3 eggs

1½ cups brewed coffee, hot

For the Filling

Butterfluff Filling (see page 255)

¼ cup cocoa powder

For the Frosting

Italian Buttercream (see page 256)

1 cup cocoa powder

For Topping

Chocolate Ganache (see page 259), warm

Chocolate, shaved

RASPBERRY PIE BARS

INGREDIENTS

2 balls of Perfect Piecrust dough
(see page 260)

3.2 oz. all-purpose flour, plus
more as needed

7 cups fresh raspberries

14 oz. sugar, plus more for
topping

2 tablespoons fresh lemon juice

Pinch of fine sea salt

1 egg, beaten

1   Preheat the oven to 350°F and coat a rimmed 15 x 10-inch baking sheet with nonstick cooking spray. Roll out one of the balls of dough on a lightly floured work surface so that it fits the baking sheet. Place it in the pan, press down to ensure that it is even, and prick it with a fork. Roll out the other crust so that it is slightly larger than the sheet.

2   Place the raspberries, sugar, flour, lemon juice, and salt in a mixing bowl and stir until well combined. Spread this mixture evenly across the crust in the baking sheet.

3   Place the top crust over the filling and trim away any excess. Brush the top crust with the egg and sprinkle additional sugar on top.

4   Place the bars in the oven and bake until golden brown, about 40 minutes. Remove from the oven and let cool before slicing.

RICE KRISPIES TREATS

INGREDIENTS

¾ lb. marshmallow creme

4½ oz. unsalted butter

¾ teaspoon fine sea salt

9 cups crispy rice cereal

¾ teaspoon pure vanilla extract

2½ cups chocolate chips or M&M's (optional)

1 Line a 13 x 9-inch baking pan with parchment paper and coat with nonstick cooking spray.

2 Fill a small saucepan halfway with water and bring it to a simmer. Place the marshmallow creme, butter, and salt in a heatproof mixing bowl over the simmering water and stir the mixture with a rubber spatula until the butter has melted and the mixture is thoroughly combined. Remove the bowl from heat, add the cereal and vanilla, and fold until combined. If desired, add the chocolate chips or M&M's and fold until evenly distributed.

3 Transfer the mixture to the baking pan and spread it with a rubber spatula. Place another piece of parchment over the mixture and pack it down with your hand until it is flat and even. Remove the top piece of parchment.

4 Place the pan in the refrigerator for 1 hour.

5 Run a knife along the edge of the pan and turn the mixture out onto a cutting board. Cut into squares and enjoy.

BAKLAVA

INGREDIENTS

1 cup plus 2 tablespoons sugar

¾ cup water

½ cup honey

1 cinnamon stick

5 whole cloves

¼ teaspoon fine sea salt

1½ cups slivered almonds

1½ cups walnuts

1 teaspoon cinnamon

¼ teaspoon ground cloves

1 lb. frozen phyllo dough, thawed

1 cup unsalted butter, melted

1   Place 1 cup of the sugar, the water, honey, cinnamon stick, whole cloves, and half of the sea salt in a saucepan and bring the mixture to a boil, stirring to dissolve the sugar. Reduce the heat and simmer until the mixture is syrupy, about 5 minutes. Remove the pan from heat and let the syrup cool. When it is cool, strain the syrup and set it aside.

2   Place the almonds in a food processor and pulse until finely chopped. Place the almonds in a bowl, add the walnuts to the food processor, and pulse and they are finely chopped. Add them to the bowl along with the cinnamon, ground cloves, and remaining sugar and salt and stir until combined. Set the mixture aside.

3   Preheat the oven to 300°F. Line a 10 x 8-inch baking pan with parchment paper. Place one sheet of phyllo in the pan and keep the remaining phyllo covered. Brush the sheet with some of the melted butter and place another sheet of phyllo on top. Repeat this four more times, so that you have a layer of 10 buttered phyllo sheets.

4   Spread 1 cup of the nut mixture over the phyllo. Top this with another layer of 10 buttered phyllo sheets, spread another cup of the nut mixture over it, and repeat.

5   Top the baklava with another layer of 10 buttered phyllo sheets. Using a serrated knife, cut the baklava into diamonds, making sure not to cut all the way through the bottom layer. Place the baklava in the oven and bake until it is golden brown, about 45 minutes, rotating the pan halfway through.

6   Remove the baklava from the oven and pour the syrup over it. Let the baklava cool completely, cut it all the way through, and enjoy.

RED VELVET CAKE

INGREDIENTS

12¾ oz. cake flour

1 oz. cocoa powder

½ teaspoon kosher salt

1 teaspoon baking soda

13.4 oz. unsalted butter, softened

14½ oz. sugar

6 eggs

1 teaspoon white vinegar

2½ oz. buttermilk

1 teaspoon pure vanilla extract

2 teaspoons red food coloring

Cream Cheese Frosting (see page 258)

1 Preheat the oven to 350°F. Line three round 8-inch cake pans with parchment paper and spray with nonstick cooking spray.

2 In a medium bowl, whisk together the flour, cocoa powder, salt, and baking soda. Set the mixture aside.

3 In the work bowl of a stand mixer fitted with the paddle attachment, cream the butter and sugar on high speed until the mixture is creamy and fluffy, about 5 minutes. Reduce the speed to low, add the eggs two at a time, and beat until incorporated, scraping down the side of the bowl with a rubber spatula between additions. Add the vinegar, beat until incorporated, and then add the dry mixture. Beat until thoroughly incorporated, add the buttermilk, vanilla extract, and food coloring and beat until they have been combined.

4 Pour 1½ cups of batter into each cake pan and bang the pans on the counter to distribute the batter evenly and remove any air bubbles.

5 Place the cakes in the oven and bake until set and cooked through, 26 to 28 minutes. Insert a cake tester in the center of each cake to check for doneness. Remove the cakes from the oven, transfer to a wire rack, and let them cool completely.

6 Trim a thin layer off the top of each cake to create a flat surface.

7 Place one cake on a cake stand, place 1 cup of the frosting in the center, and level it with an offset spatula. Place the second cake on top and repeat the process with the frosting. Place the last cake on top and spread 2 cups of the frosting over the entire cake using an offset spatula. Refrigerate the cake for at least 1 hour before slicing and serving.

APPLE PIE

INGREDIENTS

2 Perfect Piecrusts (see page 260), rolled out

3 Honeycrisp apples, peeled, cored, and sliced

3 Granny Smith apples, peeled, cored, and sliced

½ cup sugar

¼ cup light brown sugar

1½ tablespoons cornstarch

1 teaspoon cinnamon

½ teaspoon freshly grated nutmeg

¼ teaspoon cardamom

Zest and juice of 1 lemon

¼ teaspoon kosher salt

1 egg, beaten

Sanding sugar, for topping

1   Preheat the oven to 375°F. Coat a 9-inch pie pan with nonstick cooking spray and place one of the crusts in it.

2   Place the apples, sugar, brown sugar, cornstarch, cinnamon, nutmeg, cardamom, lemon juice, lemon zest, and salt in a mixing bowl and toss until the apples are evenly coated.

3   Fill the crust with the apple filling, lay the other crust over the top, and crimp the edge to seal. Brush the top crust with the egg and sprinkle sanding sugar over it. Cut several slits in the top crust.

4   Place the pie in the oven and bake until the filling is bubbly and has thickened, about 50 minutes. Remove from the oven and let the pie cool completely before serving.

APPLE PIE, SEE PAGE 203

CHOCOLATE CUPCAKES

INGREDIENTS

20 oz. sugar

13 oz. all-purpose flour

4 oz. cocoa powder

1 tablespoon baking soda

1½ teaspoons baking powder

1½ teaspoons kosher salt

1½ cups sour cream

¾ cup canola oil

3 eggs

1½ cups brewed coffee, hot

Butterfluff Filling
(see page 255)

Chocolate Ganache
(see page 259), warm

1   Preheat the oven to 350°F. Line a 24-well cupcake pan with liners.

2   In a medium bowl, whisk together the sugar, flour, cocoa powder, baking soda, baking powder, and salt. Sift the mixture into a separate bowl and set it aside.

3   In the work bowl of a stand mixer fitted with the whisk attachment, combine the sour cream, canola oil, and eggs on medium speed.

4   Reduce the speed to low, add the dry mixture, and beat until incorporated, scraping the side of the bowl with a rubber spatula as needed. Gradually add the hot coffee and beat until thoroughly incorporated. Pour about ¼ cup of batter into each cupcake liner.

5   Place the cupcakes in the oven and bake until they are baked through, 18 to 22 minutes. Insert a cake tester in the center of each cupcake to check for doneness. Remove from the oven and place the cupcakes on a wire rack until completely cool.

6   Using a cupcake corer or a sharp paring knife, carefully remove the center of each cupcake. Place 2 cups of the Butterfluff Filling in a piping bag and fill the centers of the cupcakes with it.

7   While the ganache is warm, dip the tops of the cupcakes in the ganache and place them on a flat baking sheet. Refrigerate the cupcakes for 20 minutes so that the chocolate will set.

8   Place 1 cup of the Butterfluff Filling in a piping bag fitted with a thin, plain tip and pipe decorative curls on top of each cupcake. Allow the curls to set for 10 minutes before serving.

LEMON MERINGUE PIE

INGREDIENTS

¼ cup cornstarch

¼ cup all-purpose flour

1¾ cups sugar

¼ teaspoon fine sea salt

2 cups water

4 egg yolks, lightly beaten

½ cup fresh lemon juice

1½ tablespoons lemon zest

1 oz. unsalted butter

1 Perfect Piecrust (see page 260), blind baked in a 9-inch springform pan

Swiss Meringue (see page 261)

1 Place the cornstarch, flour, sugar, and salt in a saucepan and stir until well combined. Add the water in a slow stream and stir until incorporated. Cook the mixture over medium heat, stirring occasionally, until it is thick, about 20 minutes. Remove from heat.

2 While whisking constantly, add ¼ cup of the mixture in the saucepan to the beaten egg yolks. Stir the tempered eggs into the saucepan and place it over medium-low heat.

3 Add the lemon juice, lemon zest, and butter and stir constantly until the mixture is thick enough to coat the back of a wooden spoon. Remove the mixture from heat and let it cool completely. Preheat the oven to 400°F.

4 Add the cooled filling to the baked piecrust and use a rubber spatula to smooth the top.

5 Spread the meringue over the filling and use a large spoon or a spatula to create swirled peaks. Place in the oven and bake until the peaks of meringue are light brown, about 6 minutes. Remove from the oven and let the pie cool completely before serving.

PUMPKIN PIE

INGREDIENTS

1 (14 oz.) can of pumpkin puree

1 (12 oz.) can of evaporated milk

2 eggs

6 oz. light brown sugar

1 teaspoon cinnamon

1 teaspoon ground ginger

½ teaspoon freshly grated nutmeg

¼ teaspoon ground cloves

½ teaspoon kosher salt

1 Perfect Piecrust (see page 260), blind baked

Whipped cream, for serving

1 Preheat the oven to 350°F. In a mixing bowl, whisk together the pumpkin puree, evaporated milk, eggs, brown sugar, cinnamon, ginger, nutmeg, cloves, and salt. When the mixture is smooth, pour it into the crust.

2 Place the pie in the oven and bake until the filling is just set, about 40 minutes. Remove from the oven and let the pie cool at room temperature for 30 minutes before transferring it to the refrigerator. Chill the pie for 3 hours.

3 Slice the pie, top each piece with a dollop of whipped cream, and serve.

BEIGNETS

INGREDIENTS

1½ cups milk

2 eggs

2 egg yolks

½ cup sugar

4 oz. unsalted butter, melted

2 tablespoons active dry yeast

25 oz. all-purpose flour, plus more as needed

1¼ teaspoons kosher salt

Canola oil, as needed

1 cup confectioners' sugar, for dusting

1   In the work bowl of a stand mixer fitted with the paddle attachment, combine the milk, eggs, egg yolks, sugar, and butter and beat on medium speed for 2 minutes.

2   Add the yeast, flour, and salt and beat until the mixture comes together as a dough, about 5 minutes.

3   Coat a medium heatproof bowl with nonstick cooking spray, transfer the dough to the bowl, and cover with plastic wrap. Refrigerate overnight.

4   Add canola oil to a Dutch oven until it is about 2 inches deep and warm it to 350°F over medium heat. Set a paper towel-lined baking sheet beside the stove.

5   Remove the dough from the refrigerator and place it on a flour-dusted work surface. Roll the dough out until it is ½ inch thick. Cut the dough into 2-inch squares.

6   Working in batches to avoid crowding the pot, carefully slip the beignets into the hot oil and fry, turning them once, until browned and cooked through, about 2 minutes. Transfer the cooked beignets to the baking sheet to drain and cool.

7   When the beignets have cooled, dust them generously with the confectioners' sugar and enjoy.

OATMEAL RAISIN COOKIES

INGREDIENTS

9 oz. unsalted butter, softened

6 oz. sugar

6 oz. light brown sugar

½ teaspoon kosher salt

2¼ teaspoons cinnamon

1½ teaspoons ground ginger

½ teaspoon cardamom

1 egg

¾ teaspoon pure vanilla extract

8 oz. all-purpose flour

1¼ teaspoons baking soda

10 oz. old-fashioned oats

7 oz. raisins

1. In the work bowl of a stand mixer fitted with the paddle attachment, cream the butter, sugar, brown sugar, salt, cinnamon, ginger, and cardamom on medium until the mixture is very light and fluffy, about 5 minutes. Scrape down the work bowl and then beat for another 5 minutes.

2. Reduce the speed to low and incorporate the egg, scraping down the work bowl as needed. Add the vanilla, beat to incorporate, raise the speed to medium, and beat for 1 minute.

3. Add the flour, baking soda, oats, and raisins, reduce the speed to low, and beat until the mixture comes together as a dough.

4. Scoop 2-oz. portions of the mixture onto parchment-lined baking sheets, making sure to leave enough space between the portions. Place the baking sheets in the refrigerator and let the dough firm up for 1 hour. If making the dough ahead of time, it will keep in the refrigerator for up to 2 days.

5. Preheat the oven to 350°F. Place the cookies in the oven and bake until they are lightly golden brown around the edges, 10 to 12 minutes.

6. Remove the cookies from the oven and let them cool on the baking sheets for a few minutes. Transfer them to wire racks and let them cool for another 20 to 30 minutes before enjoying.

MOLTEN LAVA CAKES

INGREDIENTS

1 cup cocoa powder, plus more as needed

3 oz. all-purpose flour

¼ teaspoon kosher salt

8 oz. dark chocolate (55 to 65 percent)

4 oz. unsalted butter

3 eggs

3 egg yolks

4 oz. sugar

Confectioners' sugar, for dusting

1 Preheat the oven to 425°F. Spray six 6-oz. ramekins with nonstick cooking spray and coat each one with cocoa powder. Tap out any excess cocoa powder and set the ramekins aside.

2 Sift the flour and salt into a small bowl and set aside.

3 Fill a small saucepan halfway with water and bring it to a gentle simmer. Place the dark chocolate and butter in a heatproof mixing bowl and place it over the simmering water. Stir occasionally until the mixture is melted and completely smooth. Remove the bowl from heat and set aside.

4 In another mixing bowl, whisk together the eggs, egg yolks, and sugar. Add the chocolate mixture and whisk until combined. Add the dry mixture and whisk until a smooth batter forms.

5 Pour approximately ½ cup of batter into each of the ramekins. Place them in the oven and bake until the cakes look firm and are crested slightly at the top, 12 to 15 minutes. Remove from the oven and let them cool for 1 minute.

6 Invert each cake onto a plate (be careful, as the ramekins will be very hot). Turn them right side up, then dust the cakes with confectioners' sugar and enjoy.

APPLE TURNOVERS

INGREDIENTS

2 apples, peeled, cores removed, chopped

¾ cup sugar

1 tablespoon fresh lemon juice

Pinch of fine sea salt

¼ cup applesauce

1 sheet of frozen puff pastry, thawed

All-purpose flour, as needed

1 teaspoon cinnamon

Sanding sugar, for topping

1. Preheat the oven to 375°F and line a baking sheet with parchment paper. Place the apples, 10 tablespoons of the sugar, the lemon juice, and salt in a food processor and pulse until the apples are minced. Strain the juice into a bowl through a fine sieve, reserve the juice, and place the solids in another small bowl. Stir in the applesauce and let the mixture sit for 5 minutes.

2. Place the sheet of puff pastry on a flour-dusted work surface and cut it into quarters. Place 2 tablespoons of the apple mixture in the middle of each quarter and brush the edges with some of the reserved liquid. Fold a bottom corner of each quarter over to the opposing top corner and crimp to seal. Place the sealed pastries in the refrigerator for 10 minutes.

3. Place the remaining sugar and the cinnamon in a small bowl and stir to combine.

4. Place the turnovers on the baking sheet and brush the tops with some of the reserved liquid. Sprinkle the cinnamon-and-sugar mixture over the turnovers, place the sheet in the oven, and bake, rotating the baking sheet halfway through, until the turnovers are golden brown, about 25 minutes.

5. Remove the turnovers from the oven, transfer them to wire racks, sprinkle sanding sugar over the top, and let the turnovers cool before enjoying.

WHOOPIE PIES

INGREDIENTS

9 oz. all-purpose flour

1.8 oz. cocoa powder

1½ teaspoons baking soda

½ teaspoon kosher salt

4 oz. unsalted butter, softened

½ lb. sugar

1 egg

1 teaspoon pure vanilla extract

1 cup buttermilk

2 cups Butterfluff Filling (see page 255)

1 Preheat the oven to 350°F and line two baking sheets with parchment paper. Sift the flour, cocoa powder, baking soda, and salt into a mixing bowl. Set the mixture aside.

2 In the work bowl of a stand mixer fitted with the paddle attachment, cream the butter and sugar on medium until the mixture is very light and fluffy, about 5 minutes. Scrape down the work bowl with a rubber spatula and then beat the mixture for another 5 minutes.

3 Reduce the speed to low, add the egg, and beat until incorporated. Scrape down the work bowl, raise the speed to medium, and beat the mixture for 1 minute.

4 Reduce the speed to low, add the vanilla and the dry mixture, and beat until it comes together as a smooth batter. Add the buttermilk in a slow stream and beat to incorporate.

5 Scoop 2-oz. portions of the batter onto the baking sheets, making sure to leave 2 inches between each portion. Tap the bottom of the baking sheets gently on the counter to remove any air bubbles and let the portions spread out slightly.

6 Place in the oven and bake until a cake tester inserted into the centers of the whoopie pies comes out clean, 10 to 12 minutes.

7 Remove the whoopie pies from the oven and let them cool completely on the baking sheets.

8 Carefully remove the whoopie pies from the parchment paper. Scoop about 2 oz. of the Butterfluff Filling on half of the whoopie pies and then create sandwiches by topping with the remaining half.

CHURROS

INGREDIENTS

Canola oil, as needed

35.25 oz. milk

81.1 oz. water

2.8 oz. sugar, plus more to taste

1.4 oz. salt

38.8 oz. "00" flour

38.8 oz. all-purpose flour

32 eggs

Cinnamon, to taste

Chocolate Ganache (see page 259), warm, for serving

1 Add canola oil to a Dutch oven until it is about 2 inches deep and warm to 350°F. Place the milk, water, sugar, and salt in a large saucepan and bring it to a boil.

2 Gradually add the flours and cook, stirring constantly, until the mixture pulls away from the side of the pan.

3 Place the mixture in the work bowl of a stand mixer fitted with the paddle attachment and beat until the dough is almost cool. Incorporate the eggs one at a time, scraping down the work bowl as needed.

4 Combine cinnamon and sugar in a shallow bowl and set the mixture aside. Place the dough in a piping bag fitted with a star tip. Pipe 6-inch lengths of dough into the hot oil and fry until they are golden brown. Place them on paper towel-lined plates to drain and cool slightly. Toss in cinnamon sugar and enjoy immediately with the ganache, or store the churros in the freezer.

5 To serve frozen churros, preheat the oven to 450°F. Remove the churros from the freezer and toss them in cinnamon sugar until coated. Place them in the oven and bake for 5 minutes. Remove, toss them in cinnamon sugar again, and serve with the ganache.

TIP: This preparation is for a big batch, most of which you will have to freeze, but you can also enjoy a few straight out of the fryer.

ECLAIRS

INGREDIENTS

17 oz. water

8½ oz. unsalted butter

1 teaspoon fine sea salt

2.4 oz. sugar

12½ oz. all-purpose flour

6 eggs

Pastry Cream (see page 262)

Chocolate Ganache (see page 259), warm

1 Preheat the oven to 425°F and line two baking sheets with parchment paper. In a medium saucepan, combine the water, butter, salt, and sugar and warm the mixture over medium heat until the butter is melted.

2 Add the flour to the pan and use a rubber spatula or wooden spoon to fold the mixture until it comes together as a thick, shiny dough, taking care not to let the dough burn.

3 Transfer the dough to the work bowl of a stand mixer fitted with the paddle attachment and beat on medium until the dough is no longer steaming and the bowl is just warm to the touch, at least 10 minutes.

4 Incorporate the eggs two at a time, scraping down the work bowl between each addition. Transfer the dough to a piping bag fitted with a plain tip. Pipe 12 eclairs onto the baking sheets, leaving 1½ inches between them. They should be approximately 5 inches long.

5 Place the eclairs in the oven and bake for 10 minutes. Lower the oven's temperature to 325°F and bake until they are golden brown and a cake tester inserted into their centers comes out clean, 20 to 25 minutes. Remove from the oven and let them cool on wire racks.

6 Fill a piping bag fitted with a plain tip with the Pastry Cream.

7 Using a paring knife, cut 3 small slits into the undersides of the eclairs and fill them with the Pastry Cream.

8 Carefully dip the top halves of the eclairs in the ganache, or drizzle the ganache over the pastries. Allow the chocolate to set before serving.

TIRAMISU

INGREDIENTS

2 cups freshly brewed espresso

½ cup plus 1 tablespoon sugar

3 tablespoons Kahlúa

4 large egg yolks

2 cups mascarpone cheese

1 cup heavy cream

30 Ladyfingers (see page 263)

2 tablespoons cocoa powder

1 Place the espresso, 1 tablespoon of sugar, and the Kahlúa in a bowl and stir to combine. Set the mixture aside.

2 Place 2 inches of water in a saucepan and bring to a simmer. Place the remaining sugar and egg yolks in a metal mixing bowl and set the bowl over the simmering water. Whisk the mixture continually until it has nearly tripled in volume, about 10 minutes. Remove from heat, add the mascarpone, and fold to incorporate.

3 Pour the heavy cream into a separate bowl and whisk until soft peaks start to form. Gently fold the whipped cream into the mascarpone mixture.

4 Place the Ladyfingers in the espresso mixture and briefly submerge them. Place an even layer of the soaked Ladyfingers on the bottom of a 9 x 13-inch baking pan. This will use up approximately half of the Ladyfingers. Spread half of the mascarpone mixture on top of the Ladyfingers and then repeat until the Ladyfingers and mascarpone have been used up.

5 Cover with plastic wrap and place in the refrigerator for 3 hours. Sprinkle the cocoa powder over the top before serving.

CLASSIC CHEESECAKE

INGREDIENTS

2 lbs. cream cheese, softened

⅔ cup sugar

¼ teaspoon kosher salt

4 eggs

1 tablespoon pure vanilla extract

1 Graham Cracker Crust
(see page 265), in a 9-inch
springform pan

1 Preheat the oven to 350°F. Bring 8 cups of water to a boil in a small saucepan.

2 In the work bowl of a stand mixer fitted with the paddle attachment, cream the cream cheese, sugar, and salt on high until the mixture is fluffy, about 10 minutes. Scrape down the side of the work bowl as needed.

3 Reduce the speed of the mixer to medium and incorporate one egg at a time, scraping down the work bowl as needed. Add the vanilla and beat until incorporated.

4 Pour the mixture into the Graham Cracker Crust, place the cheesecake in a large baking pan with high sides, and gently pour the boiling water into the baking pan until it reaches halfway up the side of the springform pan.

5 Cover the baking pan with aluminum foil, place it in the oven, and bake until the cheesecake is set and only slightly jiggly in the center, 50 minutes to 1 hour.

6 Turn off the oven and leave the oven door cracked. Allow the cheesecake to sit in the cooling oven for 45 minutes.

7 Remove the cheesecake from the oven and transfer it to a wire rack. Let it sit at room temperature for 1 hour.

8 Transfer the cheesecake to the refrigerator and let it cool for at least 4 hours before serving and slicing.

ZEPPOLE

INGREDIENTS

1½ cups all-purpose flour

1 tablespoon plus 1 teaspoon baking powder

¼ teaspoon fine sea salt

2 tablespoons sugar

2 eggs

2 cups ricotta cheese

Zest of 1 orange

1 cup milk

1 teaspoon pure vanilla extract

Canola oil, as needed

¼ cup confectioners' sugar

1   Sift the flour, baking powder, and salt into a bowl. Set the mixture aside.

2   Place the sugar and eggs in a separate bowl and whisk to combine. Add the ricotta, whisk to incorporate, and then stir in the orange zest, milk, and vanilla.

3   Gradually incorporate the dry mixture until it comes together as a smooth batter. Place the batter in the refrigerator and chill for 1 hour.

4   Add canola oil to a Dutch oven until it is about 2 inches deep and warm it to 350°F. Drop tablespoons of the batter into the hot oil, taking care not to crowd the pot, and fry until the zeppole are golden brown. Transfer the fried zeppole to a paper towel-lined plate and dust them with the confectioners' sugar. Enjoy at room temperature.

CANNOLI

INGREDIENTS

¾ lb. whole milk ricotta cheese

¾ lb. mascarpone cheese

4 oz. chocolate, grated

¾ cup confectioners' sugar, plus more for dusting

1½ teaspoons pure vanilla extract

Pinch of fine sea salt

10 cannoli shells

1 Line a colander with three pieces of cheesecloth and place it in the sink. Place the ricotta in the colander, form the cheesecloth into a pouch, and twist to remove as much liquid as possible from the ricotta. Keep the pouch taut and twisted, place it in a baking dish, and place a cast-iron skillet on top. Weigh the skillet down with two large, heavy cans and place in the refrigerator for 1 hour.

2 Discard the drained liquid and transfer the ricotta to a mixing bowl. Add the mascarpone, half of the grated chocolate, the confectioners' sugar, vanilla, and salt and stir until well combined. Cover the bowl and refrigerate for at least 1 hour. The mixture will keep in the refrigerator for up to 24 hours.

3 Line an 18 x 13-inch baking sheet with parchment paper. Fill a small saucepan halfway with water and bring it to a gentle simmer. Place the remaining chocolate in a heatproof mixing bowl, place it over the simmering water, and stir until it is melted.

4 Dip the ends of the cannoli shells in the melted chocolate, let the excess drip off, and transfer them to the baking sheet. Let the shells sit until the chocolate is firm, about 1 hour.

5 Place the cannoli filling in a plastic bag and cut a ½-inch slit in it. Pipe the filling into the shells, working from both ends to ensure they are filled evenly. When all of the cannoli have been filled, dust them with confectioners' sugar and enjoy.

MARBLE BROWNIES

INGREDIENTS

½ cup all-purpose flour, plus more as needed

½ cup unsalted butter

4 oz. milk chocolate chips

3 large eggs, at room temperature

1 cup sugar

Pinch of fine sea salt

½ lb. cream cheese, softened

½ teaspoon pure vanilla extract

1 Preheat the oven to 350°F. Coat a square, 8-inch cake pan with nonstick cooking spray and dust it with flour, knocking out any excess.

2 Fill a small saucepan halfway with water and bring it to a gentle simmer. Place the butter and chocolate chips in a heatproof bowl, place it over the simmering water, and stir until the mixture is melted and smooth. Remove the mixture from heat and let it cool for 5 minutes.

3 Place 2 of the eggs and three-quarters of the sugar in in the work bowl of a stand mixer fitted with the paddle attachment and beat on medium speed for 1 minute. Add the chocolate-and-butter mixture, beat for 1 minute, and then add the flour and salt. Beat until just combined and then pour into the prepared pan.

4 In a separate bowl, combine the cream cheese, remaining sugar, remaining egg, and vanilla. Beat with a handheld mixer on medium speed until light and fluffy. Spread on top of the batter and use a fork to stir the layers together. Place in the oven and bake for 35 minutes, until the top is springy to the touch. Remove from the oven, allow the brownies to cool in the pan, and then cut into bars.

APPENDIX

CHICKEN STOCK

INGREDIENTS

10 leftover chicken bones

32 cups cold water

¼ cup white wine

1 onion, chopped

1 celery stalk, chopped

1 carrot, chopped

2 bay leaves

10 sprigs of fresh parsley

10 sprigs of fresh thyme

1 teaspoon black peppercorns

Salt, to taste

1 Preheat the oven to 400°F. Place the chicken bones on a baking sheet, place them in the oven, and roast until they are caramelized, about 1 hour.

2 Remove the chicken bones from the oven and place them in a stockpot. Cover them with the water and bring to a boil, skimming to remove any impurities that rise to the surface.

3 Deglaze the baking sheet with the wine, scraping up any browned bits from the bottom. Stir the liquid into the stock, add the remaining ingredients, and reduce the heat so that the stock simmers. Simmer the stock until it has reduced by three-quarters and the flavor is to your liking, 6 to 8 hours, skimming the surface as needed.

4 Strain the stock and either use immediately or let it cool completely and store it in the refrigerator.

BEEF STOCK

INGREDIENTS

2 lbs. yellow onions, chopped

1 lb. carrots, chopped

1 lb. celery, chopped

5 lbs. beef bones

2 tablespoons tomato paste

16 cups water

1 cup red wine

1 tablespoon black peppercorns

2 bay leaves

3 sprigs of fresh thyme

3 sprigs of fresh parsley

1   Preheat the oven to 375°F. Divide the onions, carrots, and celery among two baking sheets in even layers. Place the beef bones on top, place the pans in the oven, and roast the vegetables and beef bones for 45 minutes.

2   Spread the tomato paste over the beef bones and then roast for another 5 minutes.

3   Remove the pans from the oven, transfer the vegetables and beef bones to a stockpot, and cover with the water. Bring to a boil.

4   Reduce the heat so that the stock simmers. Deglaze the pans with the red wine, scraping up any browned bits from the bottom. Stir the liquid into the stock, add the remaining ingredients, and cook, skimming any impurities that rise to the surface, until the stock has reduced by half and the flavor is to your liking, about 6 hours.

5   Strain the stock and either use immediately or let it cool completely before storing in the refrigerator.

CORN TORTILLAS

INGREDIENTS

1 lb. masa harina

1½ tablespoons kosher salt

3 cups warm filtered water, plus more as needed

1 In the work bowl of a stand mixer fitted with the paddle attachment, combine the masa harina and salt. With the mixer on low speed, slowly begin to add the water. The mixture should come together as a soft, smooth dough. You want the masa to be moist enough so that when a small ball of it is pressed flat in your hands, the edges do not crack. Also, it should not stick to your hands when you peel it off your palm.

2 Let the masa rest for 10 minutes and check the hydration again. You may need to add more water, depending on environmental conditions.

3 Warm a cast-iron skillet over high heat. Portion the masa into 1-ounce balls and cover them with a damp linen towel.

4 Line a tortilla press with two 8-inch circles of plastic. You can use a grocery store bag, a resealable bag, or even a standard kitchen trash bag as a source for the plastic. Place a masa ball in the center of one circle and gently push down on it with the palm of one hand to flatten. Place the other plastic circle on top and then close the tortilla press, applying firm, even pressure to flatten the masa into a round tortilla.

5 Open the tortilla press and remove the top layer of plastic. Carefully pick up the tortilla and remove the bottom piece of plastic.

6 Gently lay the tortilla flat in the pan, taking care to not wrinkle it. Cook for 15 to 30 seconds, until the edge begins to lift up slightly. Turn the tortilla over and let it cook for 30 to 45 seconds before turning it over one last time. If the hydration of the masa was correct and the heat is high enough, the tortilla should puff up and inflate. Remove the tortilla from the pan and store in a tortilla warmer lined with a linen towel. Repeat until all of the prepared masa has been made into tortillas.

YIELD: 48 WRAPPERS   •   ACTIVE TIME: 1 HOUR   •   TOTAL TIME: 3 HOURS

WONTON WRAPPERS

INGREDIENTS

¼ cup water, plus more as needed

1 large egg

¾ teaspoon kosher salt

1½ cups all-purpose flour, plus more as needed

Cornstarch, as needed

1   Place the water, egg, and salt in a measuring cup and whisk to combine. Place the flour in the work bowl of a stand mixer fitted with the paddle attachment. With the mixer running on low speed, add the egg mixture in a steady stream and beat until the mixture just comes together, adding water or flour in ½-teaspoon increments if the dough is too dry or too wet, respectively.

2   Fit the mixer with the dough hook and knead the dough on medium speed until it is soft, smooth, and springs back quickly when poked with a finger, about 10 minutes. Cover the bowl tightly with plastic wrap and let it rest for 2 hours.

3   Cut the dough into three pieces. Working with one piece at a time (cover the others tightly with plastic wrap), shape the dough into a ball. Place the dough on a flour-dusted work surface and roll it out into a rectangle that is about ½ inch thick. Feed the dough through a pasta maker, adjusting the setting to reduce the thickness with each pass, until the dough is a thin sheet, thin enough that you can see your hand through it (about 1/16 inch thick). Place the sheets on a parchment-lined baking sheet.

4   Dust a work surface with cornstarch and cut the sheets into as many 4-inch squares or 3-inch rounds as possible. Pile the cut wrappers on top of each other and fill as desired or cover with plastic wrap and store in the refrigerator for up to 3 days.

MARINARA SAUCE

INGREDIENTS

4 lbs. tomatoes, quartered

1 large yellow onion, chopped

15 garlic cloves, crushed

2 teaspoons finely chopped fresh thyme

2 teaspoons finely chopped fresh oregano

2 tablespoons extra-virgin olive oil

1½ tablespoons kosher salt

1 teaspoon black pepper

2 tablespoons finely chopped fresh basil

1 tablespoon finely chopped fresh parsley

1 Place all of the ingredients, except for the basil and parsley, in a Dutch oven and cook over medium heat, stirring constantly, until the tomatoes release their liquid and begin to collapse, about 10 minutes.

2 Reduce the heat to low and cook, stirring occasionally, for about 1½ hours, or until the flavor is to your liking.

3 Stir in the basil and parsley and season to taste. The sauce will be chunky. If you prefer a smoother texture, transfer the sauce to a blender and puree before serving.

STEAMED BUNS

INGREDIENTS

1 teaspoon active dry yeast

3 tablespoons water, at room temperature

1 cup bread flour, plus more as needed

4 teaspoons sugar

2 teaspoons nonfat dry milk powder

1 teaspoon kosher salt

⅛ teaspoon baking powder

⅛ teaspoon baking soda

4 teaspoons vegetable shortening, plus more as needed

1   Place the yeast and water in the work bowl of a stand mixer fitted with the dough hook, gently stir the mixture, and let it sit until it becomes foamy, about 10 minutes.

2   Add the remaining ingredients to the work bowl and knead the mixture on low speed until it comes together as a smooth dough, about 10 minutes. Cover the bowl with a kitchen towel and let the dough rise in a naturally warm spot until it has doubled in size, about 45 minutes.

3   Place the dough on a flour-dusted work surface and cut it into 12 pieces. Roll them into balls, cover them with plastic wrap, and let them rise for 30 minutes.

4   Cut a dozen 4-inch squares of parchment paper. Roll each ball into a 4-inch oval. Grease a chopstick with shortening, gently press the chopstick into the middle of each oval, and fold the dough over the chopstick to create a bun. Place each bun on a square of parchment paper and let them rest for 30 minutes. To cook the buns, follow the instructions in Step 3 on page 61.

OKONOMIYAKI SAUCE

INGREDIENTS

3 tablespoons Worcestershire sauce

3½ tablespoons ketchup

2 tablespoons oyster sauce

1½ tablespoons light brown sugar

1 Place all of the ingredients in a bowl and whisk until the brown sugar has dissolved and the mixture is well combined.

2 Use immediately or store in the refrigerator.

HUMMUS

INGREDIENTS

2 lbs. dried chickpeas

1 tablespoon baking soda

12 cups Vegetable Stock
(see page 249)

1 cup tahini paste

2 tablespoons za'atar

2 tablespoons sumac

2 tablespoons cumin

2 tablespoons kosher salt

2 tablespoons black pepper

2 garlic cloves, grated

½ bunch of fresh cilantro,
chopped

1 cup extra-virgin olive oil,
plus more for garnish

¼ cup sesame oil

1 cup ice water

½ cup fresh lemon juice

Paprika, for garnish

1   Place the chickpeas, baking soda, and 12 cups of room-temperature water in a large saucepan, stir, and cover. Let the chickpeas soak overnight at room temperature.

2   Drain the chickpeas and rinse them. Place them in a large saucepan, add the stock, and bring to a steady simmer. Cook until the chickpeas are quite tender, about 1 hour.

3   In a blender or food processor, combine all of the remaining ingredients and puree until achieving a perfectly smooth, creamy sauce; the ice water is the key to getting the correct consistency.

4   Add the warm drained chickpeas to the tahini mixture and blend until the hummus is perfectly smooth and not at all grainy, occasionally stopping to scrape down the side of the bowl. This blending process may take 3 minutes; remain patient and keep going until the mixture is very creamy and fluffy, adding water as necessary to get the right consistency.

5   Taste, adjust the seasoning as necessary, garnish with paprika and additional olive oil, and enjoy.

FISH STOCK

INGREDIENTS

2 lbs. fish bones

1 lb. yellow onions, finely diced

½ lb. celery, finely diced

½ lb. parsnips, peeled and finely diced

1 bay leaf

3 sprigs of fresh thyme sprigs

16 cups water

1 tablespoon black peppercorns

1   Place all of the ingredients in a stockpot and bring it to a boil.

2   Reduce the heat so that the stock simmers and cook, skimming to remove any impurities that rise to the surface, for 45 minutes.

3   Strain the stock and either use immediately or let it cool completely before storing in the refrigerator.

VEGETABLE STOCK

INGREDIENTS

2 tablespoons extra-virgin olive oil

2 large leeks, trimmed and rinsed well

2 large carrots, peeled and sliced

2 celery stalks, sliced

2 large yellow onions, sliced

3 garlic cloves, unpeeled but smashed

2 sprigs of fresh parsley

2 sprigs of fresh thyme

1 bay leaf

8 cups water

½ teaspoon black peppercorns

Salt, to taste

1 Place the olive oil and vegetables in a large stockpot and cook over low heat until the liquid they release has evaporated. This will allow the flavor of the vegetables to become concentrated.

2 Add the garlic, parsley, thyme, bay leaf, water, peppercorns, and salt. Raise the heat to high and bring to a boil. Reduce the heat so that the stock simmers and cook for 2 hours, skimming to remove any impurities that float to the surface.

3 Strain through a fine sieve, let the stock cool slightly, and place in the refrigerator, uncovered, to chill. The stock will keep in the refrigerator for 3 to 5 days, and in the freezer for up to 3 months.

BOUQUET GARNI

INGREDIENTS

2 bay leaves

3 sprigs of fresh thyme

3 sprigs of fresh parsley

1   Cut a 2-inch section of kitchen twine. Tie one side of the twine around the herbs and knot it tightly.

2   To use, attach the other end of the twine to one of the pot's handles and slip the herbs into the broth. Remove before serving.

YIELD: 8 SERVINGS • ACTIVE TIME: 15 MINUTES • TOTAL TIME: 4 HOURS

PICKLED RED ONIONS

INGREDIENTS

2 red onions, sliced thin

1 tablespoon black peppercorns

2 tablespoons kosher salt

1 cup apple cider vinegar

1 cup water

3 tablespoons sugar

1 Place the onions and peppercorns in a large mason jar.

2 Combine the salt, vinegar, water, and sugar in a saucepan and bring the mixture to a boil, stirring to dissolve the salt and sugar.

3 Pour the brine into the mason jar and let it cool to room temperature.

4 Store the pickled red onions in the refrigerator for 4 hours before serving.

SPICY BBQ SAUCE

INGREDIENTS

5 cups ketchup

1 cup brown sugar

2 tablespoons fish sauce

1 cup apple juice

1 tablespoon garlic powder

1½ teaspoons onion powder

1 tablespoon smoked paprika

1½ teaspoons cayenne pepper

1 teaspoon chili powder

1 teaspoon celery seeds

½ teaspoon cumin

1 teaspoon coriander

1 tablespoon kosher salt

1 Place all of the ingredients in a large saucepan and bring to a simmer, stirring frequently.

2 Reduce the heat to low and gently simmer the sauce, stirring occasionally, until it has thickened and the flavor has developed to your liking. Use immediately or let the sauce cool completely and store it in the refrigerator.

KIMCHI

INGREDIENTS

1 cup plus 1 tablespoon kosher salt

8 cups water, plus more as needed

7 lbs. napa cabbage, chopped

8 garlic cloves

2 oz. rice flour

1 onion, chopped

2 tablespoons minced shrimp

2-inch piece of fresh ginger, grated

¼ cup fish sauce

2 lbs. daikon radish, peeled and cut into cubes

1 bunch of scallions, trimmed and chopped

½ cup gochugaru

1 tablespoon oyster sauce

2 Granny Smith apples, grated

1 Place 1 cup of salt and the water in a large pot and stir to combine. Add the cabbage and let it soak for 3 hours.

2 Place the garlic, rice flour, onion, and shrimp in a blender and puree until smooth. Transfer the mixture to a bowl.

3 Wearing rubber gloves, drain the cabbage, rinse it well, and add it to the bowl. Add the remaining ingredients, including the remaining salt, and work the mixture with your hands, looking to both squeeze as much liquid as possible from the cabbage and to combine the mixture.

4 Transfer the mixture to mason jars, pressing down to make sure the liquid covers the kimchi entirely. If the liquid does not cover the kimchi, add water as necessary.

5 Cover each jar with a paper towel and secure it with a rubberband. Store the kimchi in a cool, dark place until the flavor has developed to your liking, 2 to 4 days. Store in the refrigerator.

HOISIN SAUCE

INGREDIENTS

2 tablespoons avocado oil

4 garlic cloves, minced

¼ cup soy sauce

3 tablespoons honey

2 tablespoons white vinegar

2 tablespoons tahini paste

2 teaspoons sriracha

1 Place the avocado oil in a saucepan and warm it over medium heat. Add the garlic and cook, stirring frequently, for 1 minute.

2 Stir in the soy sauce, honey, vinegar, tahini, and sriracha and cook until the sauce is smooth, about 5 minutes. Remove the pan from heat and let the sauce cool before using or storing in the refrigerator.

BUTTERFLUFF FILLING

INGREDIENTS

½ lb. marshmallow creme

10 oz. unsalted butter, softened

11 oz. confectioners' sugar

1½ teaspoons pure vanilla extract

¾ teaspoon kosher salt

1 In the work bowl of a stand mixer fitted with the paddle attachment, cream the marshmallow creme and butter on medium speed until the mixture is light and fluffy, about 5 minutes.

2 Add the confectioners' sugar, vanilla, and salt, reduce the speed to low, and beat for 2 minutes. Use immediately, or store in the refrigerator for up to 1 month.

ITALIAN BUTTERCREAM

INGREDIENTS

2 cups sugar

½ cup water

8 egg whites

¼ teaspoon fine sea salt

1½ lbs. unsalted butter, softened

1 teaspoon pure vanilla extract

1 Place the sugar and water in a small saucepan, fit it with a candy thermometer, and bring the mixture to a boil.

2 While the syrup is coming to a boil, place the egg whites and salt in the work bowl of a stand mixer fitted with the whisk attachment and whip on medium speed until the mixture holds stiff peaks.

3 Cook the syrup until the thermometer reads 245°F. Immediately remove the pan from heat. Once the syrup stops bubbling, let it sit for 30 seconds.

4 Reduce the speed of the mixer to medium-low and slowly pour the syrup down the side of the mixing bowl until all of it has been incorporated. Raise the speed to high and whip until the meringue is glossy and holds stiff peaks.

5 Add the butter 4 oz. at a time and whip until the mixture has thickened.

6 Reduce the speed to medium, add the vanilla, and beat until incorporated.

7 Use immediately, or store in the refrigerator for up to 2 weeks. If refrigerating, return to room temperature before using.

CREAM CHEESE FROSTING

INGREDIENTS

1 cup unsalted butter, softened

1 cup cream cheese, softened

2 lbs. confectioners' sugar

⅛ teaspoon kosher salt

¼ cup heavy cream

½ teaspoon pure vanilla extract

1   In the work bowl of a stand mixer fitted with the paddle attachment, combine the butter, cream cheese, confectioners' sugar, and salt and beat on low speed until the sugar starts to be incorporated into the butter. Raise the speed to high and beat until the mixture is smooth and fluffy, about 5 minutes.

2   Reduce the speed to low, add the heavy cream and vanilla extract, and beat until incorporated. Use immediately, or store in the refrigerator for up to 2 weeks. If refrigerating, return to room temperature before using.

YIELD: 1½ CUPS • **ACTIVE TIME:** 10 MINUTES • **TOTAL TIME:** 2 HOURS AND 30 MINUTES

CHOCOLATE GANACHE

INGREDIENTS

½ lb. chocolate (dark, milk, or white)

1 cup heavy cream

1 Place the chocolate in a heatproof mixing bowl and set it aside.

2 Place the heavy cream in a small saucepan and bring to a simmer over medium heat.

3 Pour the cream over the chocolate and let the mixture rest for 1 minute.

4 Gently whisk the mixture until thoroughly combined. Use immediately if drizzling over a cake or serving with fruit. Let the ganache cool for 2 hours if piping. The ganache will keep in the refrigerator for up to 5 days.

PERFECT PIECRUSTS

INGREDIENTS

1 cup unsalted butter, cubed

12½ oz. all-purpose flour, plus more as needed

½ teaspoon kosher salt

4 teaspoons sugar

½ cup ice water

1 Transfer the butter to a small bowl and place it in the freezer.

2 Place the flour, salt, and sugar in a food processor and pulse a few times until combined.

3 Add the chilled butter and pulse until the mixture is crumbly, consisting of pea-sized clumps.

4 Add the water and pulse until the mixture comes together as a dough.

5 Place the dough on a flour-dusted work surface and fold it over itself until it is a ball. Divide the dough in two and flatten each piece into a 1-inch-thick disc. Cover each piece with plastic wrap and place in the refrigerator for at least 2 hours before rolling out to fit your pie plate.

SWISS MERINGUE

INGREDIENTS

4 egg whites

1 cup sugar

Pinch of kosher salt

1 Fill a small saucepan halfway with water and bring it to a gentle simmer.

2 Place the egg whites, sugar, and salt in the work bowl of a stand mixer. Place the bowl over the simmering water and whisk until the mixture reaches 115°F.

3 Return the bowl to the stand mixer and fit it with the whisk attachment. Whip on high until the meringue is shiny, glossy, and holds stiff peaks, about 5 minutes. For best results, use the meringue the day you make it.

PASTRY CREAM

INGREDIENTS

2 cups whole milk

1 tablespoon unsalted butter

½ cup sugar

3 tablespoons cornstarch

2 large eggs

Pinch of fine sea salt

½ teaspoon pure vanilla extract

1 Place the milk and butter in a saucepan and bring to a simmer over medium heat.

2 As the milk mixture is coming to a simmer, place the sugar and cornstarch in a small bowl and whisk to combine. Add the eggs and whisk until the mixture is smooth and creamy.

3 Slowly pour half of the hot milk mixture into the egg mixture and stir until incorporated. Add the salt and vanilla, stir to incorporate, and pour the tempered egg mixture into the saucepan. Cook, while stirring constantly, until the mixture is very thick and about to come to a boil.

4 Remove from heat and pour the pastry cream into a bowl. Place plastic wrap directly on the surface to prevent a skin from forming. Place in the refrigerator and chill for about 2 hours before using.

LADYFINGERS

INGREDIENTS

⅔ cup all-purpose flour, plus more as needed

3 eggs, separated

½ cup plus 1 tablespoon sugar

1 teaspoon pure vanilla extract

Pinch of fine sea salt

¾ cup confectioners' sugar

1 Preheat the oven to 300°F. Line two baking sheets with parchment paper and dust them with flour.

2 Place the egg yolks in a mixing bowl and gradually incorporate the sugar, using a handheld mixer on high speed. When the mixture is thick and pale yellow, whisk in the vanilla.

3 In the work bowl of a stand mixer fitted with the whisk attachment, beat the egg whites and salt until the mixture holds soft peaks. Scoop one-quarter of the whipped egg whites into the egg yolk mixture and sift one-quarter of the flour on top. Fold to combine. Repeat until all of the egg whites and flour have been incorporated and the mixture is light and airy.

4 Spread the batter in 4-inch-long strips on the baking sheets, leaving 1 inch between them. Sprinkle the confectioners' sugar over each strip and place the ladyfingers in the oven.

5 Bake the ladyfingers until they are lightly golden brown and just crispy, about 20 minutes. Remove them from the oven and transfer the ladyfingers to a wire rack to cool completely before using.

GRAHAM CRACKER CRUST

INGREDIENTS

1½ cups graham cracker crumbs

2 tablespoons sugar

1 tablespoon real maple syrup

3 oz. unsalted butter, melted

1 Preheat the oven to 375°F. Place the graham cracker crumbs and sugar in a large mixing bowl and stir to combine. Add the maple syrup and 5 tablespoons of the melted butter and stir until thoroughly combined.

2 Grease a 9-inch pie plate with the remaining butter. Pour the crumb mixture into the pie plate and gently press into shape. Line the crust with aluminum foil, fill it with uncooked rice, dried beans, or pie weights, and bake for about 10 minutes, until the crust is firm.

3 Remove from the oven, remove the aluminum foil and chosen weight, and allow the crust to cool completely before filling. This process is known as blind baking.

METRIC CONVERSIONS

U.S. Measurement	Approximate Metric Liquid Measurement	Approximate Metric Dry Measurement
1 teaspoon	5 ml	5 g
1 tablespoon or ½ ounce	15 ml	14 g
1 ounce or ⅛ cup	30 ml	29 g
¼ cup or 2 ounces	60 ml	57 g
⅓ cup	80 ml	76 g
½ cup or 4 ounces	120 ml	113 g
⅔ cup	160 ml	151 g
¾ cup or 6 ounces	180 ml	170 g
1 cup or 8 ounces or ½ pint	240 ml	227 g
1½ cups or 12 ounces	350 ml	340 g
2 cups or 1 pint or 16 ounces	475 ml	454 g
3 cups or 1½ pints	700 ml	680 g
4 cups or 2 pints or 1 quart	950 ml	908 g

INDEX

ABOUT CIDER MILL PRESS BOOK PUBLISHERS

❋ ❋ ❋

Good ideas ripen with time. From seed to harvest,
Cider Mill Press brings fine reading, information,
and entertainment together between the covers of its
creatively crafted books. Our Cider Mill bears fruit twice
a year, publishing a new crop of titles each spring and fall.

"Where Good Books Are Ready for Press"
501 Nelson Place
Nashville, Tennessee 37214

cidermillpress.com